Learning VMware vCloud Air

Leverage VMware's latest public cloud offering to build an efficient hybrid cloud infrastructure for your business

Yohan Rohinton Wadia

BIRMINGHAM - MUMBAI

Learning VMware vCloud Air

First published: July 2015

Production reference: 1270715

Published by Packt Publishing Ltd.
Livery Place
35 Livery Street
Birmingham B3 2PB, UK.

ISBN 978-1-78528-287-4

www.packtpub.com

Credits

Author
Yohan Rohinton Wadia

Reviewers
Anil Gupta (AJ)
Ram Pradyumna Rampalli

Commissioning Editor
Ashwin Nair

Acquisition Editor
Vinay Argekar

Content Development Editor
Gaurav Sharma

Technical Editors
Rohith Rajan
Rupali Shrawane

Copy Editors
Yesha Gangani
Vikrant Phadke

Project Coordinator
Bijal Patel

Proofreader
Safis Editing

Indexer
Rekha Nair

Production Coordinator
Melwyn D'sa

Cover Work
Melwyn D'sa

About the Author

Yohan Rohinton Wadia is a client-focused virtualization and cloud expert with over 5 years of experience in the IT industry. He has been involved in conceptualizing, designing, and implementing large-scale solutions for a variety of enterprise customers. These were based on the VMware vSphere, VMware vCloud, and Amazon Web Services platforms.

He has authored numerous articles on cloud computing and open source technologies and products in international magazines, such as *Open Source For You* and *Ezine*. Yohan has also coauthored and published an IEEE paper titled *Portable Autoscaler for Managing Multi-Cloud Elasticity*. He shares his passion for technology on his blog at http://www.yoyoclouds.com.

He is currently working with Virtela Technology Services, an NTT communications company. He is involved in managing the company's in-house cloud platform, and he works on various open source and enterprise-level cloud solutions for internal as well as external customers. He is a VMware Certified Professional and a vExpert (2012 and 2013) as well.

Acknowledgments

I wish to dedicate this book to both my loving parents, Ma and Paa. Thank you for all your love, support, encouragement, and patience—I know you need a lot of it when dealing with me! I would also like to extend my thanks to my best buddy and brother, Mitesh Soni, who not only taught me blogging and authoring but has also been a strong source of moral support and guidance ever since.

I would also like to thank the entire Packt Publishing team, especially Hemal Desai and Gaurav Sharma, for their excellent support, guidance, and patience. Last but not least, a special few who also made a difference towards the completion of this book in their own ways are Karthic Kumar, Nikhil Madhava, Dave Fitzjarrell, and Yashvardhan Vyas. Thank you for all your support.

And finally, to someone who really made a big difference in my life—my knight in shining black armour. Miss you a lot, my Xena. Wish you were here.

"Lost, but not forgotten"

About the Reviewers

Anil Gupta (AJ) works as a technology consultant for VMware's System Engineering (Presales) team, which supports the Sales function of VMware. He is a vExpert 2014 and an active member of the VMware community. His industry experience includes working in a wide range of roles, such as system administration, architecture, consultancy, sales, presales, product marketing, partner management, team leadership, support, training, and software testing. Apart from VMware, he has worked with organizations such as Hewlett Packard, Avaya, and IGate.

In his current role, Anil is an expert in business development around virtualization and cloud solutions. He does this by helping customers identify the right and optimized solution for their infrastructure. He has implemented complex designs and incorporated his clients' existing infrastructure and applications. Anil has superior knowledge of formulating business sense to technology, which he also shares with the virtualization community on his blog at `http://www.walkonblock.com`. He has spoken at many events, such as VMworld, vFORUM, Partner Exchange, and various industry-leading events.

First and foremost, I would like to thank the author, Yohan Rohinton Wadia, for not only writing this amazing book, but also giving me an opportunity to be part of it.

Then, I would like to thank my parents, friends, and colleagues at VMware for their love and support.

Special thanks to Murad Wagh, the senior manager of VMware, for his mentorship and the encouragement that made me venture into new ideas.

I am also grateful to Bijal Patel from Packt Publishing for her continuous support during the review.

Ram Pradyumna Rampalli is a Technical Support Engineer at VMware and provides support for wide range of VMware Virtualization and Cloud solutions.

He has 4 years of experience in the technical industry, for a year and a half of which he worked at Avaya Telecommunications. For the rest of the period, he worked on VMware virtualization and cloud support.

I would like to thank Bijal Patel at Packt Publishing, who is the project coordinator of this book. She has been very cooperative throughout the review phase and all the hurdles that came along with it.

I would also like to express my gratitude and give thanks to my elder brother, Prathyush Ram Rampalli, for all the motivation and encouragement for this project.

My heartfelt thanks to the Packt Publishing team for giving me an opportunity to review this book.

www.PacktPub.com

Support files, eBooks, discount offers, and more

For support files and downloads related to your book, please visit www.PacktPub.com.

Did you know that Packt offers eBook versions of every book published, with PDF and ePub files available? You can upgrade to the eBook version at www.PacktPub.com and as a print book customer, you are entitled to a discount on the eBook copy. Get in touch with us at service@packtpub.com for more details.

At www.PacktPub.com, you can also read a collection of free technical articles, sign up for a range of free newsletters and receive exclusive discounts and offers on Packt books and eBooks.

https://www2.packtpub.com/books/subscription/packtlib

Do you need instant solutions to your IT questions? PacktLib is Packt's online digital book library. Here, you can search, access, and read Packt's entire library of books.

Why subscribe?
- Fully searchable across every book published by Packt
- Copy and paste, print, and bookmark content
- On demand and accessible via a web browser

Free access for Packt account holders

If you have an account with Packt at www.PacktPub.com, you can use this to access PacktLib today and view 9 entirely free books. Simply use your login credentials for immediate access.

Instant updates on new Packt books

Get notified! Find out when new books are published by following @PacktEnterprise on Twitter or the *Packt Enterprise* Facebook page.

Table of Contents

Preface

VMware vCloud Air is a public cloud platform built on the VMware vSphere and the VMware vCloud Director platforms. It provides Infrastructure-as-a-Service (IaaS) on a pay-per-use subscription model. Currently, it provides three types of services for its customers, namely Dedicated Cloud, Virtual Private Cloud, and Disaster Recovery.

VMware vCloud Air has come a long way from its early inception in 2013 as vCloud Hybrid Service. It wasn't until August 2014 that vCloud Hybrid Service was rebranded as vCloud Air. Today, vCloud Air has made its presence felt globally by having world-class data centers across the United States, Europe, Asia, and Australia. Using these data centers, customers can extend their on-premise infrastructure to vCloud Air by leveraging a host of VMware products and services, such as direct connect, vCloud connector, VMware NSX services, and so on. This provides a lot of flexibility and agility to organizations that are looking to actively expand their resources, but do not want to invest heavily in infrastructure startups. And now with vSphere 6 launched, VMware is actively looking to integrate its management, operations, and automations suite of products with vCloud Air, thus making it easy for enterprise customers to leverage and extend their existing on-premise portfolio of applications to vCloud Air.

This book will provide you with a step-by-step guide to and, hands-on learning experience with VMware vCloud Air. With easy-to-follow instructions, ample screenshots to refer to, and a host of best practices and tips, it will give you a practical understanding that will help you get started with VMware vCloud Air.

What this book covers

Chapter 1, Getting Started with VMware vCloud Air, introduces the concepts and features of cloud computing. This chapter discusses the importance of cloud computing and how it can be leveraged to bring competitive advantages to businesses. It provides an introduction to vCloud Air, its components, and its features, and tells you how to get started with its services.

Chapter 2, Working with Virtual Machines, covers the basics of virtual machines, vApps, templates, and catalogs. It describes in detail how you can create and launch your own set of virtual machines in vCloud Air. The chapter also describes a few essential best practices and tips that you should keep in mind when designing and building your virtual machines on the vCloud Air platform.

Chapter 3, vCloud Air Networking and Security, delves into the concepts of networking, with a special emphasis on gateways, DHCP services, network address translation, load balancing, and so on. This chapter also provides you with a step-by-step guide that will help you connect your virtual machines with the outside world.

Chapter 4, Extending vCloud Air, focuses on the different types of connectivity options provided by VMware vCloud Air to customers for extending their on-premise data centers to the cloud. The chapter also provides an in-depth look at the VPN service and tells you how you can leverage it to connect vCloud Air with other VMware-backed private and public clouds. Then it covers the basics of installing and using VMware vCloud Connector as a tool to migrate your workloads from an on-premise environment to the vCloud Air platform.

Chapter 5, Monitoring Workloads on vCloud Air, covers a basic overview of the VMware vRealize suite of products, with a special emphasis on VMware vRealize Operations Manager. This chapter describes in detail how to deploy a fully functional vRealize Operations Manager into your on-premise VMware environment, and leverage it to monitor your workloads on VMware vCloud Air.

Chapter 6, Business Continuity and Disaster Recovery using vCloud Air, describes the importance of a good and functional disaster recovery plan. This chapter also provides an in-depth view of VMware vCloud Air's disaster recovery service, its components, and its key features. It walks you through simple steps to configure vSphere replication with vCloud Air and test and perform virtual machine replications.

What you need for this book

This book assumes that you have basic to intermediate knowledge and hands-on experience with VMware products, including the VMware vSphere and vCloud Director platforms. A basic understanding of cloud computing and its delivery models and key benefits will also be beneficial here. You will, furthermore, need Internet access and the latest version of either Google Chrome or Firefox to access the vCloud Air environment. You will also require the latest copy of Putty Manager or any other such SSH tool for obtaining remote sessions of your Linux virtual machines on the vCloud Air platform. Although not required, it is beneficial to have either a working VMware vSphere-based lab set up in your on-premise environment. There are a plenty of tutorials out there on the Internet that can guide you through how to create a mini-VMware lab on a laptop. This will come in handy when integrating vCloud Air with products such as VMware vCloud Connector, vRealize Operations Manager, vSphere Replications, and so on.

Who this book is for

This book is aimed at beginners, system administrators, cloud developers, and cloud administrators who are on the path to learning and leveraging VMware vCloud Air as a public cloud for their organization.

Conventions

In this book, you will find a number of styles of text that distinguish between different kinds of information. Here are some examples of these styles, and an explanation of their meaning.

Code words in text, database table names, folder names, filenames, file extensions, pathnames, dummy URLs, user input, and Twitter handles are shown as follows: " To log in to the virtual machine, use the following credentials:

- Username: root
- Password: <Guest_OS_Password>"

A block of code is set as follows:

```
<html>
<body bgcolor="black"><font color="white">
<center><h1>This is HTTP PROD SERVER 1</h1></center>
</font></body>
</html>
```

Any command-line input or output is written as follows:

```
# yum install httpd
```

New terms and **important words** are shown in bold. Words that you see on the screen, in menus or dialog boxes for example, appear in the text like this: "Once the form is filled in, simply click on the **Submit** button."

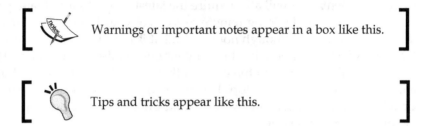

Warnings or important notes appear in a box like this.

Tips and tricks appear like this.

Reader feedback

Feedback from our readers is always welcome. Let us know what you think about this book—what you liked or may have disliked. Reader feedback is important for us to develop titles that you really get the most out of.

To send us general feedback, simply send an e-mail to feedback@packtpub.com, and mention the book title via the subject of your message.

If there is a topic that you have expertise in and you are interested in either writing or contributing to a book, see our author guide on www.packtpub.com/authors.

Customer support

Now that you are the proud owner of a Packt book, we have a number of things to help you to get the most from your purchase.

Downloading the color images of this book

We also provide you a PDF file that has color images of the screenshots/diagrams used in this book. The color images will help you better understand the changes in the output. You can download this file from: http://www.packtpub.com/sites/default/files/downloads/2874EN_ColorImages.pdf

Errata

Although we have taken every care to ensure the accuracy of our content, mistakes do happen. If you find a mistake in one of our books—maybe a mistake in the text or the code—we would be grateful if you would report this to us. By doing so, you can save other readers from frustration and help us improve subsequent versions of this book. If you find any errata, please report them by visiting http://www.packtpub.com/submit-errata, selecting your book, clicking on the **errata submission form** link, and entering the details of your errata. Once your errata are verified, your submission will be accepted and the errata will be uploaded on our website, or added to any list of existing errata, under the Errata section of that title. Any existing errata can be viewed by selecting your title from http://www.packtpub.com/support.

Piracy

Piracy of copyright material on the Internet is an ongoing problem across all media. At Packt, we take the protection of our copyright and licenses very seriously. If you come across any illegal copies of our works, in any form, on the Internet, please provide us with the location address or website name immediately so that we can pursue a remedy.

Please contact us at copyright@packtpub.com with a link to the suspected pirated material.

We appreciate your help in protecting our authors, and our ability to bring you valuable content.

Questions

You can contact us at questions@packtpub.com if you are having a problem with any aspect of the book, and we will do our best to address it.

1

Getting Started with VMware vCloud Air

Imagine being able to kick start your new business with a simple click of a mouse button; imagine having the ability to scale IT infrastructure up and down dynamically, all with a few clicks, while you only pay for what you use and not a penny more! This is just part of the essence and power that cloud computing can provide today.

Cloud computing has definitely evolved a lot over the years. It is not surprising that today, it has become almost a mainstream part of our lives; from storing personal data and accessing it from anywhere across the world, to having burst compute capacity and enterprise software applications available on demand, anytime and anywhere.

A lot of top-notch companies are already investing heavily in cloud computing for the future, building a variety of open source and propriety cloud tools, and platforms that we, as end users, can use and exploit to the fullest. One such company is **VMware**, which has been a leader in the virtualization industry for quite some time. VMware offers a huge suite of enterprise class products that can be leveraged to transform your IT datacenters into fully functional and automated cloud environments. In this book, we are going to explore the possibilities of cloud computing using VMware's latest service offering in the Public Cloud arena called **VMware vCloud Air**.

In this chapter, we are going to look at some of the features and benefits provided by Cloud Computing in general, along with a few interesting enterprise use cases for cloud computing. We will be covering this through the following topics:

- What is cloud computing what are its uses?
- Components and concepts of vCloud Air
- vCloud Air Service Offerings
- Signing up for VMware vCloud Air

Later on, we will look into some simple steps that will help you sign up and get started quickly with VMware vCloud Air.

What is cloud computing?

The obvious question that must be lingering in your minds by now is, "what's all the talk and buzz about cloud computing? What does it really have to offer?"

Let's have a quick look at what exactly cloud computing is.

NIST or the National Institute of Standards and Technology defines cloud computing as *A model for enabling ubiquitous, convenient, on-demand network access to a shared pool of configurable computing resources (for example, networks, servers, storage, applications, and services) that can be rapidly provisioned, and released with minimal management effort or service provider interaction.*

It also talks about certain essential characteristics of cloud computing that are worth mentioning:

- **Resource pooling**: One of the key features of cloud computing is the ability to pool resources, and make them available to users on demand in a shared fashion. In simpler terms, the users are abstracted from the complexities of the underlying hardware, or the location of the servers and the datacenters. All that is required is for users to log into the cloud portal, provision, and de-provision resources on the fly.
- **Multi-tenancy**: A common characteristic of a cloud is its ability to provide shared services to multiple end users. This style of providing a shared service from a common resource while keeping the user-specific data isolated is called multi-tenancy.

- **Cost effective**: Because of pooling resources and multi-tenancy, there is very little wastage of resources in a cloud environment. Hardware and software come precompiled and are ready to use a format that reduces the overall costs of deployment, management, and operation as well. Besides these, most public cloud vendors also offer their services on a utility style costing, thus eliminating the need for any upfront payments or heavy investments.

- **Pay-as-you-go model**: The utility style of costing makes sure that the cloud users only pay for the resources that they use, and not a penny more. This helps them to keep track of their resource consumptions and billing as well, while eliminating wastage of unnecessary resources.

- **Robust and reliable**: Clouds run off multiple datacenters; most of them geographically isolated from each other. The idea here is that in case one server, multiple servers, or even an entire rack fails, the cloud service would still run unaffected from it. This is due to a lot of built-in redundancy and automated fault tolerance. In some cases, where a cloud draws its resource from multiple data centers and an entire datacenter should go offline, individual cloud users would still suffer no outages. There is, in other words, no single point of failure, which would make a public cloud service vulnerable.

- **Flexible services**: Clouds today provide a very large set of services for the users to choose from, ranging from **IaaS (Infrastructure as a Service)**, to **PaaS (Platform as a Service)**, and even **SaaS (Software as a Service)**. These services can be accessed via the Internet, enabled and consumed on demand, and then shut down and disposed of as well, once your tasks are over. Major business today even integrate their services with public clouds using open source APIs, thus forming hybrid clouds: special sets of clouds that can provide the pros of both private and public cloud computing while eliminating their individual cons.

Now that we have a basic understanding of what a cloud is, and some of its features and benefits, let's look at some interesting enterprise-level cases of where a cloud can be used.

How is cloud computing useful?

- **Burst compute capacity**: An organization has to compute and process a lot of payroll information towards the end of each month. This processing requires compute power; the more the power the faster the results are calculated. Cloud computing can provide such burst compute capacity on demand to its users, when they need it the most. The organization can spin up **virtual machines** or **instances** in the cloud, scale them based on the randomness of their demand, and then destroy all the instances once the job is done. This entire process can also be automated to make the entire payroll computation far easier and effective at the end of each month's cycle.

- **Dev and Test**: A classic use case when it comes to cloud computing is the development and testing of applications and code on the cloud. Organizations can host their development centers on-premises and test the applications on the cloud by spinning up instances quickly, testing on them, and then tearing the entire infrastructure back down when not needed. Massive and complex infrastructure environments can be built on clouds with ease with the use of templates, cloning, and automated provisioning.

- **Disaster recovery**: A common use case for most enterprises today is to use a cloud as a mechanism for disaster recovery. Organizations create stand-by infrastructure environments on a cloud that can either perform hot or cold migrations on demand. Clouds today use a variety of techniques to achieve this such as live virtual machine replication, templates, and cloning.

- **Temporary sites**: Similar to the development and test scenario, a cloud can also be used to spin up simple advertising, marketing web sites, or a micro-site for a couple of months. Organizations can easily create and power on entire sites in the cloud, use it for a certain amount of time, and then tear it all down (and save it potentially for later use) once they are done.

vCloud Air – concepts and components

Now that we have seen what cloud computing is, and what its features and benefits are, let's dive into the crux of the book itself by introducing VMware vCloud Air.

VMware vCloud Air is basically a public cloud platform that is built on two of VMware's flagship products: the virtualization and consolidation engine called VMware vSphere, and the multi-tenant cloud platform called **VMware vCloud Director**.

Organizations can run their existing workloads as well as launch new apps and services on VMware vCloud Air with ease, thus allowing them the freedom and flexibility to extend their existing datacenters into the cloud.

vCloud Air service offerings

VMware vCloud Air offers three types of service offerings for the end users, each with its own preconfigured and preallocated amount of compute, storage, and network resources to begin with. These resources are just a starting point and can be extended as per the user's requirements.

The types of vCloud Air services

The vCloud Air service offerings are broadly classified into three main categories: **Dedicated Cloud**, which provides a single tenant virtual private cloud for the end user; the **VMware vCloud Air Virtual Private Cloud**, which is more of a multi-tenant virtual private cloud, and can be used by multiple organizations; and last but not least, **Disaster Recovery**, which provides seamless **DR** options from premises to the cloud and vice versa.

The following image shows the types of vCloud Air Services:

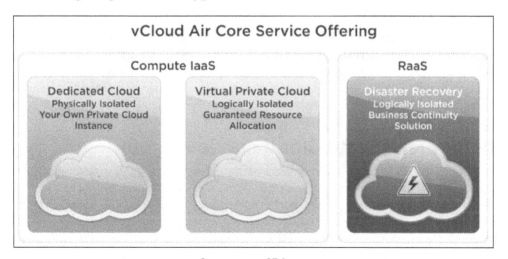

Image source: VMware

The Dedicated Cloud service

The Dedicated Cloud service provides a single tenant private cloud with dedicated computing servers, layer-2 network isolation for workload traffic, persistent storage volumes, and a dedicated cloud management instance. Think of it as your own rack, servers, storage, and networks. There is no multi-tenancy here. This type of dedicated infrastructure is best suited for organizations that have really sensitive data, and don't wish to share infrastructure with any other organization; for example, banks and government organizations would generally go with a dedicated cloud service.

The dedicated cloud service provides users with more control and flexibility of how the resources are used and administered. Think of a dedicated cloud as your own private cloud hosted in a public cloud.

Table 1 – Dedicated Cloud service capacities:

Service Component	Capacity
Computer	120 GB vRAM, 30GHz vCPU
Storage	6TB standard or accelerated storage
Bandwidth	50 Mbps
Public IP addresses	3 included + optional
Production support	24 x 7 x 365

Each dedicated cloud service comes with a starter pack of the information mentioned in the preceding table; however, users are not limited to that capacity only. Dedicated cloud users can extend their capacities as per their requirement anytime by simply logging in to their VMware account and purchasing additional resources on demand.

The Virtual Private Cloud service

The Virtual Private Cloud service works in a similar way as the dedicated cloud service. The only difference is that the underlying physical resources are shared between multiple customers. An important point to remember here is that although the physical infrastructure is shared, it is logically isolated and provided to individual customers, thus providing an illusion that they were running on dedicated resources directly. This logical isolation has no performance impact to the customers, as the resources are dedicated and made available on demand whenever required.

Table 2 – Let us have a quick look at a Virtual Private Cloud's service capacities:

Service Component	Capacity
Compute	20 GB vRAM, 5GHz vCPU burstable up to 10GHz
Storage	2TB standard or accelerated storage
Bandwidth	10 Mbps
Public IP addresses	2 included + optional
Production support	24 x 7 x 365

The Disaster Recovery service

Disaster Recovery or **Recovery-as-a-Service (RaaS)** is a new service offering provided by vCloud Air, which is intended to take backups, and protect your virtualized infrastructure, whether it is hosted on the vSphere or vCloud Director environment.

This service enables users to manage and protect their virtual infrastructure by asynchronously replicating the virtual machines from a source site; say, your local vSphere environment to the cloud for recovery.

Table 3 – Disaster recovery (RaaS) service capacities:

Service Component	Capacity
Compute	20 GB vRAM, 10GHz vCPU
Storage	1TB standard storage
Bandwidth	10 Mbps
Public IP addresses	2 included + optional
Production support	24 x 7 x 365

 As a vSphere customer, or vSphere and vCloud Air customer, you will need to contact your VMware sales representative to purchase a vCloud Air – Disaster Recovery subscription.

vCloud Air relies on two of the VMware's products to perform disaster recovery, and a brief about each is as follows:

vSphere Replication

vSphere Replication is a part of the vSphere product suite that enables users to replicate and automate the failover of their virtual machines to remote sites, such as vCloud Air. An important thing to note here is that vSphere Replication does not support automatic failback of virtual machines; that is, vSphere Replication does not move the virtual machines from vCloud Air back to the on-premises vSphere environment automatically. This is a manual process.

vCloud Connector

vCloud Connector is a free tool provided by VMware, and is used to connect your on-premises vSphere environment with a remote VMware vCloud. vCloud Connector is a useful tool when it comes to migrating templates and virtual machines from an internal private cloud to a public cloud.

Signing up for VMware vCloud Air

Signing up for VMware vCloud Air is a fairly simple process. At the time of writing this book, VMware has set up an **Early Access Program (EAP)**. If you are a new user and interested in the EAP, then simply sign up for the program at `http://vcloud.vmware.com/service-offering/virtual-private-cloud-ondemand`.

The link takes you to a short questionnaire. Once the form is filled in, simply click on the **Submit** button. You will receive an email at the email address that you provided during the sign-up process. This email will contain a link and a temporary password to create an account on vCloud Air. Click on the link to get started:

1. If you already have a My VMware Account, then simply login by providing your email address and password under **LOG IN/CREATE ACCOUNT**, or you can optionally create a new My VMware account.

   The following screenshot shows the VMware vCloud Air OnDemand Services log-in/sign-up page:

2. Enter your credit card and billing information and click on **Complete Sign-Up**. You can optionally provide a different billing address as well if required.

The following screenshot shows the page where you fill in the credit card and billing information:

3. Once VMware has validated your account information, you will receive a confirmation email that will provide you with a URL to access your vCloud Air along with a few other necessary account activation instructions.

4. Navigate to the given URL and set a new password for accessing your account. Always use a strong password, and remember to check the **I accept** checkbox before you click on **Continue**.

   The following screenshot shows the VMware vCloud Air password setup screen:

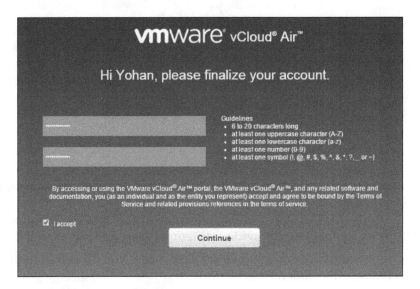

5. Provide your username and password and click on **Sign in** to begin using your vCloud Air subscription. You will be prompted to accept VMware vCloud Air's terms and conditions. Simply click on **Submit** and continue.

For subsequent logins, go to `https://vca.vmware.com` and log in using your username and password.

The following screenshot shows the VMware vCloud Air log-in screen:

6. Once logged in, you will see vCloud Air's main dashboard, as shown in the following screenshot:

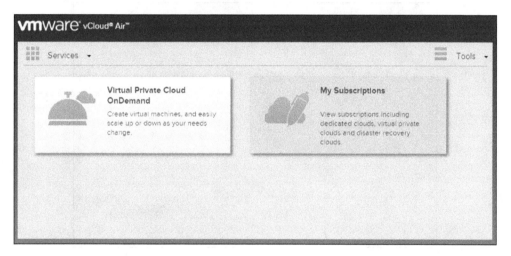

Here, you can see that VMware has already provided you with an On-Demand vCloud service. Get started by selecting the **Virtual Private Cloud On-Demand**. This will bring up a dialog box that will allow you to select the default **Region** out of which you will operate.

Regions

Regions are a collection of one or more physical datacenters that can be geographically separated from each other. Users can select any region in VMware vCloud Air to get started. However, a good choice will be to select the region that's closest to you.

Why provide a choice of regions? Well, failures can happen, and hosting all your workloads in a single datacenter is not a best practice. Having your workloads available in multiple regions allows users to deploy highly redundant and fault tolerant applications, which can work even if one entire datacenter goes down. Having multiple regions also means that you can run your workloads a lot closer to where your customers reside, and at the same time, comply with various local legal regulations and laws.

The following screenshot shows the VMware vCloud Air **Virtual Private Cloud OnDemand** region selection screen:

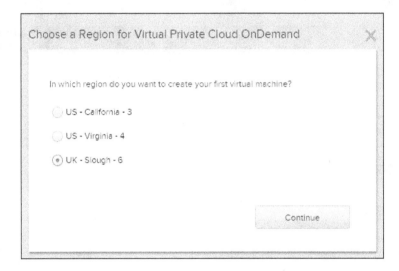

In this case, VMware vCloud Air is showing three regions, two in the US and one in UK. For the purpose of this guide, I have selected the UK region (**UK - Slough - 6**), but you can always go back and change this using the vCloud Air dashboard.

Navigating through the interface

Once you have selected your region, you will see the main dashboard, as shown previously. This is the starting point for all your vCloud Air activities. Let's have a quick look into what each tab is going to be used for; first up is the **Resource Usage** tab.

Resource usage

As the name implies, the resource usage tab displays historic as well as real-time usage of your cloud's resources. You can even view detailed reports for up to a month using this console.

The following screenshot shows the VMware Private Cloud OnDemand **Resource Usage** tab:

 You will not be charged for any resources unless you start using them. The following console views the estimate costs to date of each of your resources.

If you want an in-depth usage and cost report, then log in to your **My VMware** account and traverse to **Services | Subscription Service Detail**, as shown:

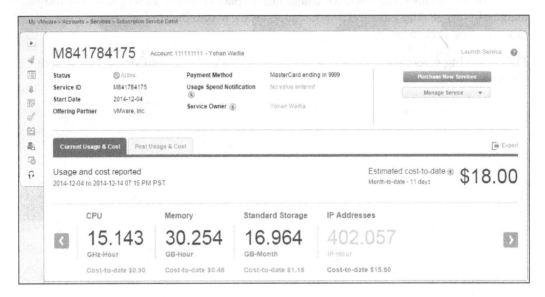

Virtual machines

A virtual machine is a software-based computer which, as a physical computer, runs on a host operating system. Virtual machines are first-class objects in vCloud Air interactions, and you can manage them individually.

Using the virtual machines tab, you can create, edit, delete and view all your virtual machines or instances. By default, vCloud Air provides a list of readymade templates including CentOS, Ubuntu, and Windows Server OSs, with which you can create your own instances; however, you can also create or upload your own custom templates and ISO images, and spawn instances from them. This will be covered in depth in the subsequent chapters.

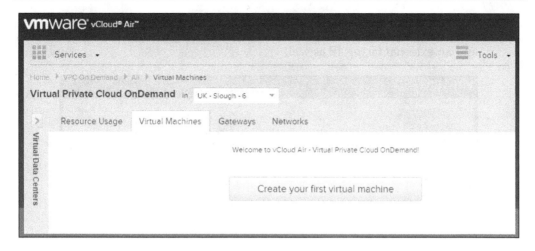

Gateways

The vCloud Air uses **Software Defined Networking (SDN)** concepts and technology for creating and using networking elements, such as gateways and routers.

The gateway in vCloud Air is basically responsible for routing traffic to and from your internal vCloud environment to the outside world, that is, the Internet.

When you subscribe to a Virtual Private Cloud service, VMware creates your virtual data center for you, and adds a gateway to that virtual data center, as it's done in this case. When you subscribe to a Dedicated Cloud service, you have to log in to the vCloud Air console, and create your first virtual data center. When you allocate a public IP address range to your virtual data center, vCloud Air creates a gateway in that virtual data center.

By default, a gateway provides the following properties:

- **Small footprint**: a gateway doesn't use much disk or compute resources
- **High availability**: by default, this feature is disabled, but you can enable it by using VMware vCloud Director

- **IP Networks**: by default, the gateway will provide you with an internal network (generally a 192.168.xxx.xxx series IP range with a default gateway), and an external facing IP as well

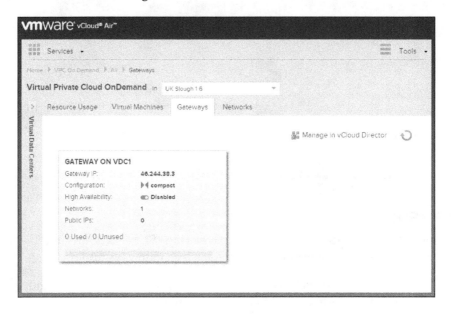

A gateway provides additional services, such as firewall, NAT, DHCP VPN, and load balancing as well, each of which will be explored in depth in the subsequent chapters.

> By default, all the services mentioned above are set to be disabled. So, when you assign a virtual machine to the default gateway, it will not provide any connectivity to the outside world. In order for the virtual machine to get internet connectivity, you will have to open up the relevant ports and enable NAT as well on the gateway, so that the internal (192.168.xxx.xxx) IP address of the VM is translated into the external (gateway) one.

Networks

The **Networks** tab displays the overall networks that can be consumed by the virtual machines in a vCloud Air environment. There are two types of networks that can be created here:

- **Default-Routed-Network**: this network is used to connect your instances with the outside world.

- **Isolated Network**: as the name implies, this is an isolated network. It does not contain any edge gateway to route traffic to the outside world.

The following screenshot shows the VMware vCloud Air **Networks** tab:

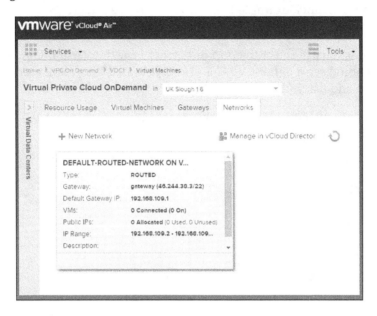

Both the default-routed and isolated networks use a range of internal IP addresses. These IP addresses can be viewed in the vCloud Air dashboard itself by selecting the particular network that you want to view.

 Unlike the default-routed network, the isolated network does not come with a host of add-on services like load balancing and NAT; it only supports DHCP.

Virtual Datacenters – VDCs

VDCs are a mechanism by which users can isolate particular applications, and application groups by providing them dedicated compute, storage, and network resources that are logically carved up from underlying physical resources. For example, an organization typically has internal departments, such as development, testing, production, and HR. vCloud Air can create VDCs for each of these departments in such a way that the cloud administrator can create and track resource utilization for each department, and bill them based on their resource consumptions.

Using vCloud Air, you can perform a lot of management activities on a VDC, such as create VDCs, assign the maximum number of virtual machines that each VDC can support, assign dedicated routed and internal networks and storage, and so on.

Let's run through a quick example to see how easily we can create a VDC using the vCloud Air interface.

On the main dashboard, select the pop-out arrow near the **Virtual Data Centers** option. You should see a default VDC is already created for you named **VDC1**. You can create and list multiple VDCs using this this console itself.

The following screenshot shows the VDC created by default under the **Virtual Machines** tab:

To create your own VDC, click on the **+** sign next to the **Virtual Data Centers** option. This will display the following popup window. Provide a suitable name for your new VDC and click on **Create Virtual Data Center** when done.

Blank spaces in your VDC name are not allowed, so use a hyphen or an underscore in its place.

The following screenshot shows the **New Virtual Data Center** page:

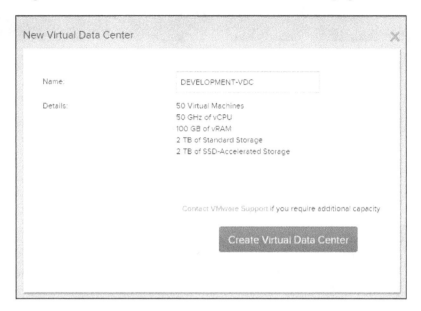

As you can see from the preceding screenshot, the VDC is created with a predefined set of resources allocated to it, such as 50 GHz of CPU, 100 GB of vRAM, and so on. You can contact the VMware support team if you wish to add more resources to your VDC.

Once created, you can list your VDCs as we did in the earlier steps. An important point to remember here is always remember to select your VDCs first, and then create virtual machines, or perform any changes to your environment.

Virtual machines created now will be specific to the VDCs, but if you wish to list all the VMs from your environment, then simply select the **All** option under the **Virtual Data Centers** drop-down list.

 Each VDC that you create will have its own default routed-gateway and isolated network created as well, so make sure you are editing or deleting the correct networks from the correct VDC.

The following screenshot shows the VDC that you just created:

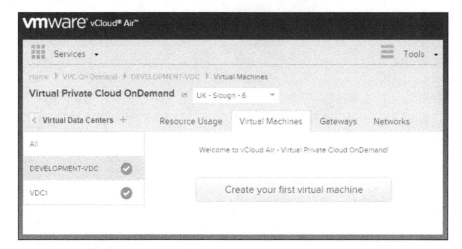

Deleting a VDC is also a simple process. Simply right-click on the VDC's name and select the option to delete.

 Deleting a VDC will free up all the resources currently allocated to it including gateways, networks and virtual machines.

Deleting a VDC

User management

VMware vCloud Air provides a simple **Identity Access Management (IAM)** portal. By using it you can create users, and assign them individual roles.

There are five specialized sets of roles provided by vCloud Air; they are summarized as follows:

- **Virtual infrastructure administrator**: they are a kind of super administrator. They have the privileges to add and modify VDCs and virtual machines. They can also view gateways, networks, activity logs, and list other users.

- **Account administrator**: they can only add users and reset passwords. Account administrators can view VDCs and their contents as well.

- **Network administrator**: this is a special role that is designed to only create and manage the networking infrastructure of your VDC, which includes routed-gateways, isolated networks, and so on. Network administrators can also view virtual data centers, virtual machines, activity logs, and users.

- **Subscription administrator**: they can manage user accounts in **My VMware**, and have permission to file support requests.

- **Read-only administrator**: they can view VDCs, virtual machines, and networks, and can list other users, but cannot alter settings in the administration areas.

Now that we understand the specific administrative roles provided by vCloud Air, let's quickly add a new user to our infrastructure.

On the main dashboard, select the **Tools** tab and under it, select the **Users** option, as shown:

Click on the **Add User** option. This will pop up the following screen on which you can create your user and assign him the required roles that we discussed previously. Provide the first and last name, and also a valid email address for your user. Once done, simply select the **Add User** option.

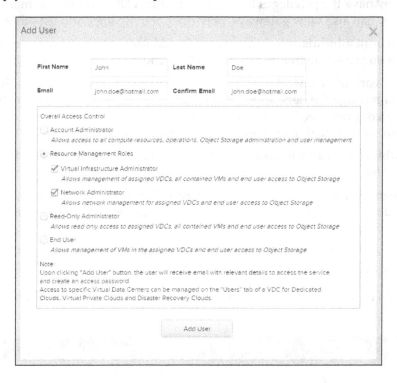

Once the user is provisioned, you can choose to enable or disable it; reset the user's password, and then even delete the user using the same console, as shown:

Summary

Let's have a quick round up of the things that we have seen so far. First, we looked at what cloud computing actually is, and at some of the basic features and benefits that you can obtain by using it. We then learned a bit about vCloud Air and its components and service models. We also saw how easy it is to sign up and get started with the **On Demand Virtual Private Cloud service**.

In the next chapter, we will be learning the basics of working with virtual machines, or instances, using VMware vCloud Air.

2

Working with Virtual Machines

In *Chapter 1, Getting Started with VMware vCloud Air*, we looked at some of the core functionalities and benefits provided by cloud computing. We also discussed the various components of VMware vCloud Air, and saw how easy it is to get started with it. In this chapter, we are going to walk through the following topics:

- What are virtual machines, vApps, templates, and catalogs
- Getting started with virtual machines, creating, editing and managing them
- Meter usage and monitoring the performance of your virtual machines

What is a virtual machine?

Most of you who are reading this book must be aware of what a virtual machine is, but for the sake of simplicity, let's have a quick look at what it really is.

A virtual machine is basically an emulation of a real or physical computer, which runs on an operating system, and can host your favorite applications as well. Each virtual machine consists of a set of files that governs the way the virtual machine is configured and run. The most important of these files is a virtual drive, which acts as a physical drive, storing all your data, applications, and operating system; and a configuration file that basically tells the virtual machine how much resources are dedicated to it, and which networks or storage adapters to use and so on. The beauty of these files is that you can port them from one virtualization platform to another, and manage them more effectively and securely, compared to a physical server.

Every virtual machine contains a guest operating system as well, which can be anything from a native Linux OS like CentOS, RedHat, Ubuntu, SUSE, and so on to a full blown Windows Server. These operating systems function just as they would on a real physical computer, as their functioning is encapsulated by the virtual machine. Once the OS is installed, you can deploy your favorite applications and services on them, just as you would on a normal server.

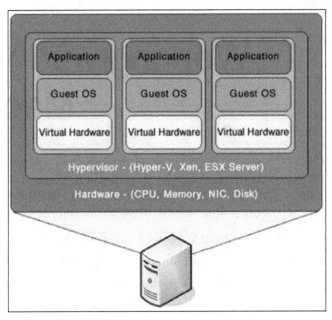

Working principle of a virtual machine

Virtual machine creation in vCloud Air is a very simple and straight-forward process. The vCloud Air application provides you with three mechanisms by which you can create your own virtual machines briefly, which are summarized as follows:

- **Wizard-driven**: vCloud Air provides a simple wizard with which you can deploy virtual machines from preconfigured templates. This option is provided via the vCloud Air web interface itself.

- **Using vCloud Director:** vCloud Air provides an advanced option as well for users who want to create their virtual machines from scratch. This is done via the vCloud Director interface and is a bit more complex than the wizard-driven option.

- **Bring your own media:** Because vCloud Air natively runs on VMware vSphere and vCloud Director platforms, it's relatively easy for you to migrate your own media, templates, and vApps into vCloud Air using a special tool called VMware vCloud Connector.

We will explore all these methods later on in this chapter, but first let's clear out some common concepts and nomenclature first.

vApps, templates, and catalogs

Now that we understand what a virtual machine is, let's look at some of the other important nomenclature that we will be coming across in this chapter and for the remainder of the book:

- **vApps**: A vApp is VMware terminology, and generally means a preconfigured and packaged virtual machine that contains an operating system, and a preinstalled application; for example, a CentOS-based virtual machine with Apache web server packages rolled into it, a Debian-based MySQL server, or a Windows 2012 server with a preconfigured DNS and DHCP roles in it are all what we call a vApp.

  vApps can also be ported from one VMware vSphere-based environment to another due to the fact that all vApps operate on the **Open Virtualization Format (OVF)**. This enables administrators to easily manage and migrate vApps from an on-premise VMware environment over to the vCloud Air.

- **Templates:** A template, also called a **golden image**, is a complete and ready-to-use blueprint of a virtual machine that can be used by administrators to clone and deploy several other copies of virtual machines from it. vCloud Air uses the concept of templates as well, where the end users are provided with a set of preconfigured and ready-to-use golden images from which a user can copy and create multiple clones. Some templates provided by vCloud Air are free of charge, whereas others have some minor licensing charge built into them. We will be deploying our first virtual machines in vCloud Air later using such a template.

- **Catalogs**: A catalog in VMware vCloud Air is basically a collection of templates that you can consume on an on-demand basis. A default catalog is provided to users when they first log in to the vCloud Air portal. This catalog contains a few Linux-based distros along with Windows Server templates as well. This catalog changes frequently as new templates become available. Alternatively, you can even create your own catalogs and publish them in vCloud Air using the vCloud Director portal. We will be looking at a few simple steps to create your own custom catalogs later in this chapter.

VMware provides a large catalog of vApps and templates at an online marketplace called **Solutions Exchange**. You can purchase preconfigured and ready-to-use apps, such as Microsoft SQL Server 2012 edition, F5 Load Balancing solution, and a lot more from here, and directly import them to your vCloud Air catalog for use at `https://solutionexchange.vmware.com/store/category_groups/vcloud-air`.

Getting started with virtual machines

Now that we have seen and understood exactly what vApps, templates, and catalogs are, let's get started by actually deploying some virtual machines on the VMware vCloud Air platform. Virtual Machines can be deployed from either predefined and configured templates that are provided by vCloud Air, or by creating your virtual machine from scratch as well. Let's have a look at both the techniques in the following sections.

Creating a virtual machine using a template

As we saw earlier, VMware vCloud Air provides us with a default template with which you can deploy virtual machines in your public cloud in a matter of seconds. The process is a wizard-driven activity, where you can select and configure the virtual machine's resources, such as CPU, memory, and hard disk space, all with a few simple clicks.

The following steps will help you create a virtual machine using a template:

1. Log in to your vCloud Air (`https://vchs.vmware.com/login`) using the username and password that we set during the sign in process.

2. From the **Home** page, select the **VPC on Demand** tab. Once there, from the drop-down menu above the tabs, select your **region** and the corresponding **VDC**, where you would like to deploy your first virtual machine.

3. In this case, I have selected the **UK-Slough-6** as the region and **MyFirstVDC** as the default VDC, where I will deploy my virtual machines.

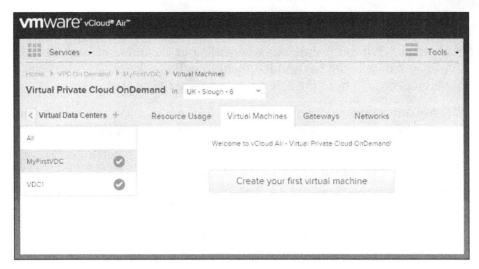

Creating a virtual machine

 If you have selected more than one VDC, you will be prompted to select a specific virtual data center before you start the wizard, as a virtual machine cannot span regions or VDCs.

4. From the **Virtual Machines** tab, select the **Create your first virtual machine** option. This will bring up the VM launch wizard as shown next:

As you can see here, there are two tabs provided by default: a **VMware catalog**, and another section called **My Catalog**. This is an empty catalog, by default, but this is the place where all your custom templates and vApps will be shown if you have added them from the vCloud Director portal, or purchased them from the Solutions Exchange site as well.

5. Select any template to get started with. You can choose your virtual machine to be either powered by a 32-bit, or a 64-bit operating system. In my case, I have selected a CentOS 6.4 64-bit template for this exercise. Click on **Continue** once done.

> Templates provided by vCloud Air are either free or paid. The paid ones generally have a **$** sign marked next to the OS architecture, indicating that you will be charged once you start using the virtual machine. You can track all your purchases using the vCloud Air billing statement.

6. The next step is to define the basic configuration for your virtual machine. Provide a suitable name for your virtual machine. You can add an optional description to it as well.

7. Next, select the CPU, memory, and storage for the virtual machine. The CPU and memory resources are linked with each other, so changing the CPU will automatically set the default vRAM for the virtual machine as well; however, you can always increase the vRAM as per your needs. In this case, the virtual machine has two CPUs and 4 GB vRAM allocated to it.

8. Select the amount of storage you want to provide for your virtual machine. VMware can allocate a maximum of 2 TB of storage as a single drive to a virtual machine. However, as a best practice, it is always good to add more storage by adding multiple drives rather than storing it all on one single drive.

> You can optionally select your disks to be either standard or SSD-accelerated; we will discuss both features shortly.

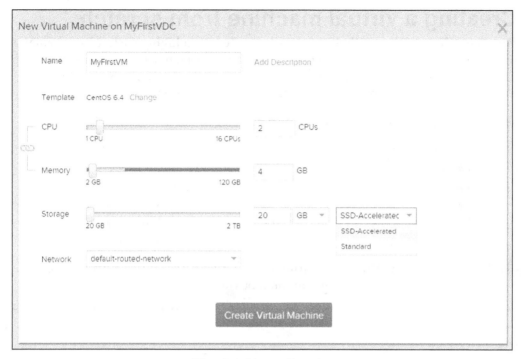

Virtual machine configuration

9. Click on **Create Virtual Machine** once you are satisfied with your changes. Your virtual machine will now be provisioned within a few minutes.

10. By default, the virtual machine is not powered on after it is created. You can power it on by selecting the virtual machine and clicking on the **Power On** icon, in the tool bar above the virtual machine.

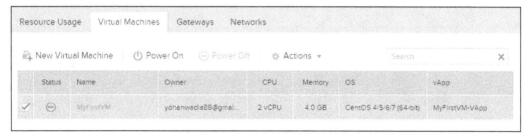

Status of the virtual machine created

There you have it. Your very first virtual machine is now ready for use! Once powered on, you can select the virtual machine name to view its details, along with a default password that is autogenerated by vCloud Air.

Creating a virtual machine from scratch

For users who wish to use their own media and create a highly customized virtual machine, vCloud Air provides an option to create virtual machines from scratch. This is accomplished by using VMware vCloud Director Portal; however, the final virtual machine will also show up in the vCloud Air dashboard.

The following steps will help you create a virtual machine:

1. Log in to your vCloud Air (`https://vchs.vmware.com/login`) using the username and password that we set during the sign in process.

2. From the **Home** page, select the **VPC on Demand** tab. Once there, from the drop-down menu above the tabs, select your **Region** and the corresponding VDC that you would like to deploy your first virtual machine.

3. Select the **Create Virtual Machine** tab as we did in the earlier steps.

4. From the **New Virtual Machine** wizard, select **Create My Virtual Machine From Scratch** option as highlighted below:

5. This will redirect you to another tab on your browser and automatically log you in to a VMware vCloud Director Portal. From the portal, select the **Build a new vApp** icon to get started.

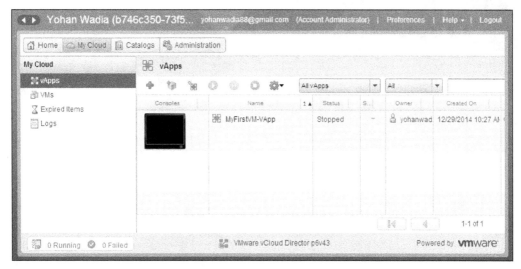

Building a vApp

6. Provide a suitable **Name** and an optional **Description** for your vApp. This vApp can contain multiple virtual machines within itself, but for the sake of simplicity, we will only be creating a single VM for now. Click on **Next** to continue.

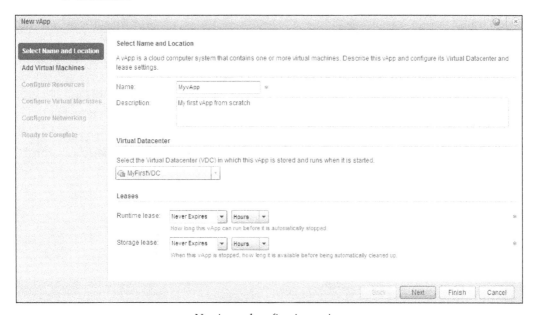

Naming and configuring a vApp

7. From the **Add Virtual Machines** wizard, select the **New Virtual Machine** icon to get started, as shown:

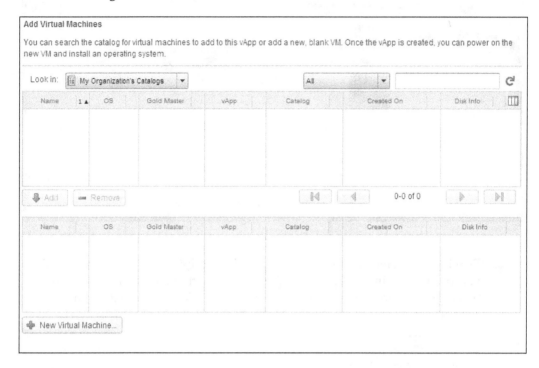

8. The following dialog will help you create your virtual machine from scratch. Most of the settings are pretty straight-forward, including the **Virtual Machine Name** and **Description** options. The **Computer name** is the default hostname that will be provided to the virtual machine when it powers **ON**:

   ° You can also select which **Virtual hardware version** you want the virtual machine to run on; by default, it is set to **HardwareVersion 10** as shown:

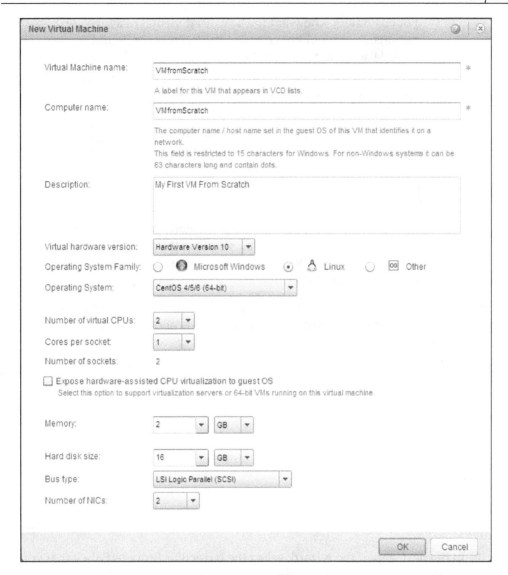

- ° Next, select **Operating System Family**. This is broadly divided into three categories: Windows, Linux, and Other.

- ° Select the appropriate **Operating System** for your virtual machine. As you will notice here, there is a lot more variety of operating systems to choose from, as compared to the default VMware catalog. This is because VMware felt the need to keep things simple and easy for its customers by providing them a standard set of operating systems that they would normally use.

- ° For customers who want the advanced virtual machine creation options, they would have to use the VMware vCloud Director console as we are doing right now.

- ° You can also provide values for **vCPU** and **vRamvRAM**, (memory) based on your custom requirements.

 NOTE: The important thing to note here is that there is no linkage between the CPU core and the amount of vRAM here, unlike the vCloud Air configuration setting that we performed earlier.

- ° You can even provide more than one network card for your virtual machine using this console by selecting the **Number of NICs**, as shown next. Click on **OK** once you are satisfied with your configuration changes.

9. This will bring you back to the **Add Virtual Machines** wizard, as shown next. Select your newly created virtual machine and then click on **Next** to proceed.

Name	OS	Gold Master	vApp	Catalog	Created On	Disk Info
VMfromScratch	CentOS 4/5/6 (64-bit)	--				16.00 GB

➕ New Virtual Machine...

Back | Next | Finish | Cancel

10. In the next step of the wizard, select the particular **Storage Policy** that you would like your virtual machine to run on. VMware provides two storage policies as of now: a standard storage, and an SSD-accelerated storage. Both will be discussed in brief in the coming chapters.

Selecting SSD-accelerated storage will incur additional costs.

Selecting a VM Storage Policy

11. Configure the networking for your virtual machine as well. In our case, we provided two NIC cards during the virtual machine creation process, hence the two NICs as shown in the following screenshot:

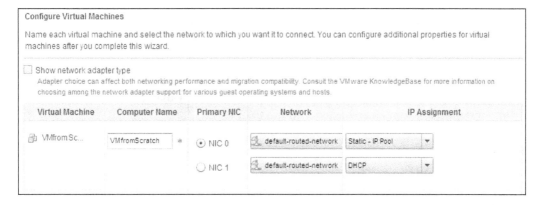

Two NIC devices configured in a virtual machine

You can opt which NIC will be the primary NIC for your virtual machine, and also select the **Network** and the type of **IP Assignment** that you wish to provide. By default, you will only have one network created and that is the **Default-routed-Network**, which is created by VMware during the initial signup phase. The IP assignment field too will only show you a default value of **Static – IP Pool**, as shown. We can create DHCP pools as well, but this will be covered in the later chapters.

12. Click on **Next** to proceed.

13. In the final **Summary** page, as shown, verify all your settings and configurations. Click on **Finish** when done.

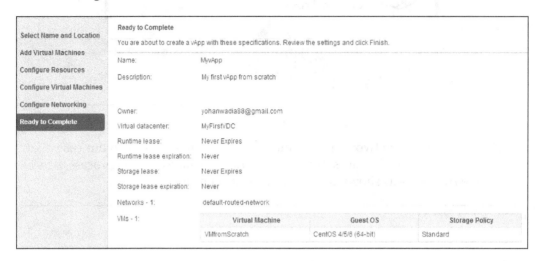

14. This will start deploying a blank virtual machine. The creation process takes about a few seconds and once completed, you will see your virtual machine created and displayed as shown next:

The same virtual machine will also be displayed on the vCloud Air's virtual machines dashboard page.

The virtual machine power operations

Once you have created your virtual machines, you can now perform power operations on them. But before we see how, let's learn the power options provided by vCloud Air.

 Advanced power options, such as **Suspend** and **Resume**, work well when the virtual machine has VMware Tools installed on it. By default, the templates provided by VMware all have VMware Tools installed and preconfigured on it.

The following table will take you through the power operations for a virtual machine:

State	Description
Power On	Powers ON a virtual machine.
Suspend/ Resume	Suspends a running virtual machine by freezing its state. Suspending a VM does not power off the VM. It preserves the virtual machine's state. You can resume from a suspended virtual machine. When resuming the virtual machine is powered back on and restored to its last state.
Reset	Power cycles the virtual machine. Resetting the virtual machine clears the memory and cache, equivalent to a reboot command for a physical machine.
Power OFF	Powers off a virtual machine.

To power on a virtual machine, follow either of the steps performed next:

1. Select the virtual machine that you wish to power on.
2. Click on the **Power On** option provided in the menu bar, above the virtual machine.
3. Select the virtual machine that you wish to power on.

4. Click on the **Action** tab and select the **Power on** option from there, as shown

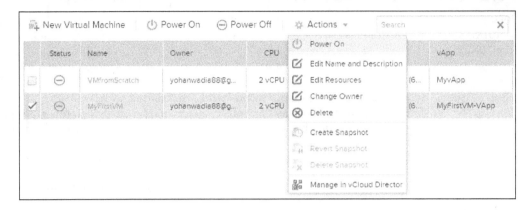

5. Once powered on, you can then **Suspend/ Resume** and power off your virtual machines in a similar way, as shown:

 You can only incur charges when your virtual machine is in a power on state.

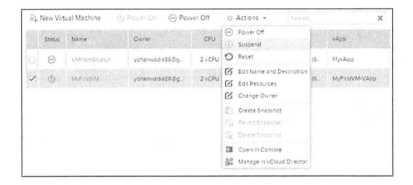

VMware vCloud Air provides users with the basic and advanced virtual machine editing options, such as changing the name, description, owner, and resources at a given point in time.

Editing the virtual machine properties using vCloud Air

By using the vCloud Air portal, you can change the properties of a virtual machine by selecting the particular virtual machine that you wish to modify. Click on the **Actions** tab and select the appropriate parameter that you wish to change:

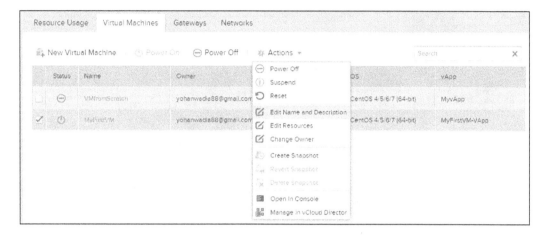

- **Change name and description**: You can edit the name and description of a virtual machine either when it is powered on or off. Simply select **Edit Name and Description** from the **Actions** tab and provide new and suitable values, as required.

 Changing the name and description of a virtual machine does not require a reboot.

Editing VM name and Description

- **Edit resources**: vCloud Air also allows you to add and remove resources from your virtual machines only when they are in a powered-off state. Simply select the **Edit Resources** from the **Actions** tab. This will bring up the following dialog, as shown:

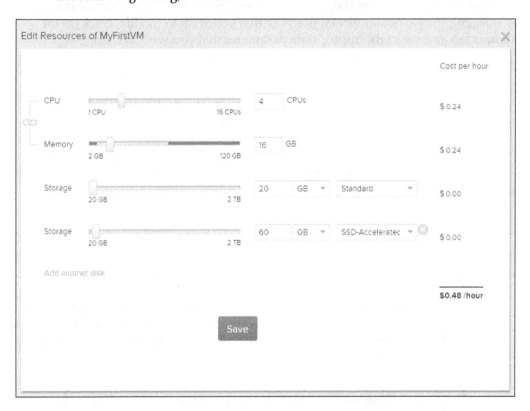

You can increase or decrease the CPU and memory resources as required. In this case, we have increased the CPUs from 2 to 4, and bumped up the memory from 4 GB to 16 GB.

You can also add an additional disk drive to your virtual machine using this dialog. Simply select the **Add another disk** option. It will add an additional disk, as shown in the previous screenshot. You can either choose this disk to be a standard drive, or an SSD-accelerated dive.

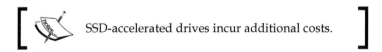 SSD-accelerated drives incur additional costs.

Once your changes are made, click on the **Save** option to finalise the configuration changes.

Editing the virtual machine properties using vCloud director

VMware vCloud also provides an easy way for editing and managing your resources using the vCloud Director UI.

Each resource can be individually configured and managed; for instance, you can create and edit DHCP server pools, build load balancers, create custom catalogs for hosting your own virtual machines, and a lot more using the vCloud Director interface.

In this exercise, we are going to use one of our previously created virtual machines, and edit its properties using the vCloud Director UI.

To begin with, select any virtual machine of your choice from the vCloud Air dashboard, as shown. Click on **Actions** tab and select the **Manage in vCloud Director** tab as shown:

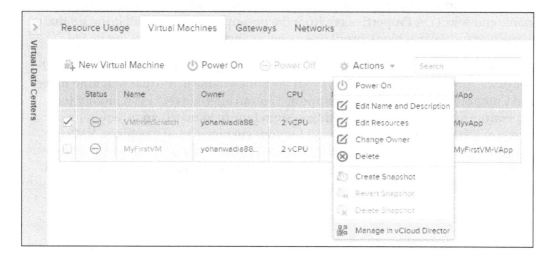

This will open a separate window tab in your browser, and will automatically log you in to a vCloud Director UI. Here, you will be redirected automatically to your virtual machine tab, as shown in the following screenshot, where you will be able to edit its properties, and set advanced options for it, which wouldn't be possible using the vCloud Air UI.

To edit the virtual machine's properties, simply right-click on the virtual machine's name and select the **Properties** tab from the pop-up menu. This will bring up that particular virtual machine's properties page, as shown in the following image.

Here, in the **General** tab, you can edit a lot of the virtual machine's settings directly, for examples you can change the virtual machine's name in **Virtual Machine name**, the **Computer name** and its **Description**. You can alternatively even modify the **Operating system** and the **Operating system family** to match your requirements. You can install VMware Tools as well for your custom virtual machines. VMware Tools are basically drivers and must be present in your virtual machine at all times. This can be installed by powering on the virtual machine and selecting the **Install VMware Tools** option from the context menu.

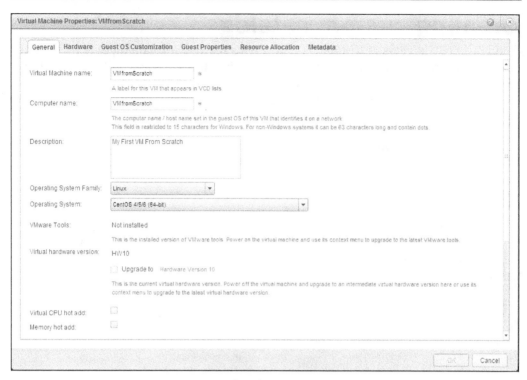

Virtual machine properties

The same also applies for the **Hardware** Tab, where you can alter the virtual machine's CPU and memory, add more disk drives to it, as well as change some of the networking parameters based on your requirements.

The **Guest OS Customization** tab is a bit new, and is really important, as here, you can enable guest OS level customization for your virtual machines, such as specifying a local administrator password when the machine boots up, and prompting the user to change the password after the first login attempt. These options are basically not provided in your default vCloud Air interface. In a vCloud Air dashboard, you will be provided with an autogenerated password, which you can use to login to your virtual machine. Also, by using the guest OS customization tab, you can even optionally add your virtual machine to a domain, and execute some custom scripts as well during the boot time. These scripts can be used to perform a wide variety of actions and functions, such as automatically mounting virtual drives to your VM, making an incremental backup of your disks, performing some software operations, and many more.

Creating custom catalogs

Previously, we have used VMware vCloud Air's readymade catalog of templates to spin up our virtual machines. As a cloud administrator, you can create and publish your custom catalogs to vCloud Air as well. Let's now look at some easy options that will help you to create your very own catalogs.

Catalogs are a means to share and provide virtual machine templates to end users. VMware vCloud Air provides a default catalog by which you can deploy readymade templates in your virtual datacenter, but you can also create and deploy your own custom virtual machines using your very own catalogs. These catalogs are created and populated using the VMware vCloud Director UI only.

To create your own catalog, select the **Manage in vCloud Director** option from the vCloud Air dashboard. You will be automatically logged in to a vCloud Director UI. From the context menu, on the right-hand side of the UI, select **New Catalog**, as shown here:

This will bring up a wizard that will help you create a blank catalog. Start by providing a suitable **Name** for your catalog. You can provide an optional description for it as well. Once the contents are filled, click on **Next** to continue, as shown:

In the next section, you will be prompted to select **Storage Type**. Selecting the correct storage type is very important, as all your virtual machines created using this catalog will be governed by the storage policy that you select here. You can either choose to use the available storage provided by your organization, or you can select a specific one. In this example, we have decided to provide only the **standard** storage policy for our catalog.

> You can either select the standard or the SSD-accelerated storage policies from the drop-down, as shown here:

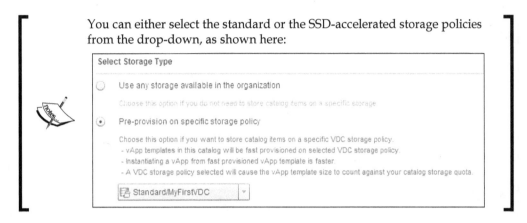

For example, you can create different catalogs for each storage policy, and make them available for a specific set of VDCs as well; create a golden image catalog that contains an SSD-accelerated storage as a default policy, and assign this catalog to the production team VDC.

The next section allows you to share your catalog by assigning users to it. This is an optional step and can be skipped if you wish to keep your catalog private. In this case, we have assigned a user to this catalog, and provided it with full control administrative rights.

You can either provide full control, read/ write, or read only rights to the catalog users. Click on **Next** to continue, as shown:

The final screen will display the summary of your settings. Click on **Finish** to create your catalog. You can list your newly created catalog, under the **Catalogs** tab, in the vCloud Director interface, as shown next. Each catalog can contain vApp templates and media files that you can share with other users in the organization. Media files include operating system ISO images that can be used to install guest operating systems on custom-made virtual machines that have been created from scratch.

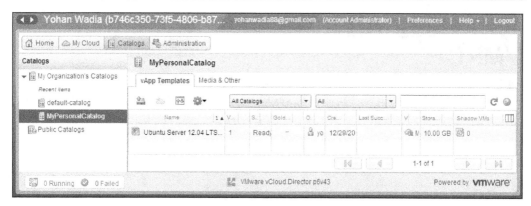

Virtual machine catalogs

You can also move vApp templates and media files from one catalog to another. Simply right-click on the item that you wish to copy or move from the catalog, and select the **Copy to Template** option. You can select any other existing catalog to copy the item over to.

In the example that we discussed higher up, we have already copied an Ubuntu Server 12.04 vApp template from VMware's default catalog over to our newly created one. The same vApp template is even visible in the vCloud Air dashboard as well. You can view it by selecting the **My Catalog** tab in the **New Virtual Machine** wizard as shown:

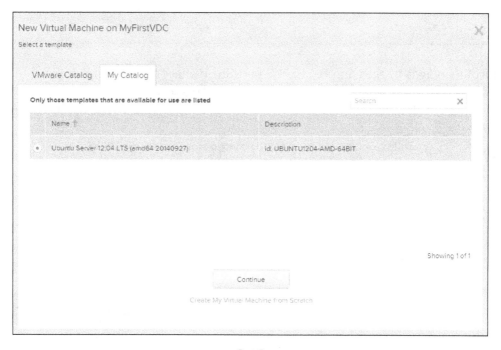

Accessing virtual machines using the VMRC

Once your virtual machines are created and powered on, you can access and view them easily using the **virtual machine remote console (VMRC)**. There are two ways to invoke the VMRC; one way is by selecting your virtual machine from the vCloud Air dashboard, selecting the **Actions** tab and selecting the option **Open in Console**, as shown:

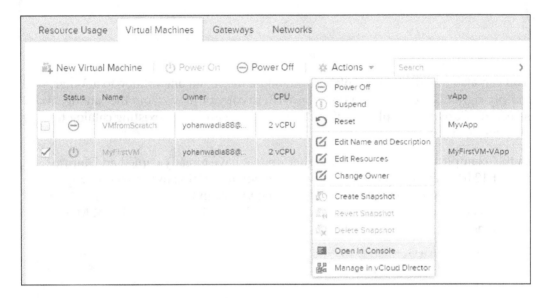

The other way is by selecting the virtual machine name. This will display the **Settings** page for that particular virtual machine. To launch the console, select the **Open Virtual Machine** option as shown:

 Make a note of **Guest OS password** from the **Guest OS** section. This is the default password that will be used to log in to your virtual machine.

MyFirstVM

This is my First VM and I have edited this comment now!!

Resource Usage   Settings   Networks

Manage in vCloud Director   ▣ Open Virtual Machine

General

Status:	Powered On
Owner:	yohanwadia88@gmail.com change
vApp:	MyFirstVM-VApp
OS:	CentOS 4/5/6/7 (64-bit)
VMware Tools:	enabled

Resources edit

CPU:	2
Memory (GB):	4
Storage (GB):	20 (Standard)

Guest OS

Guest OS Customization:	on
Guest OS Password:	4kE%#%oB

To log in to the virtual machine, use the following credentials:

- Username: root
- Password: <Guest_OS_Password>

The following screenshot shows the console terminal of the virtual machine:

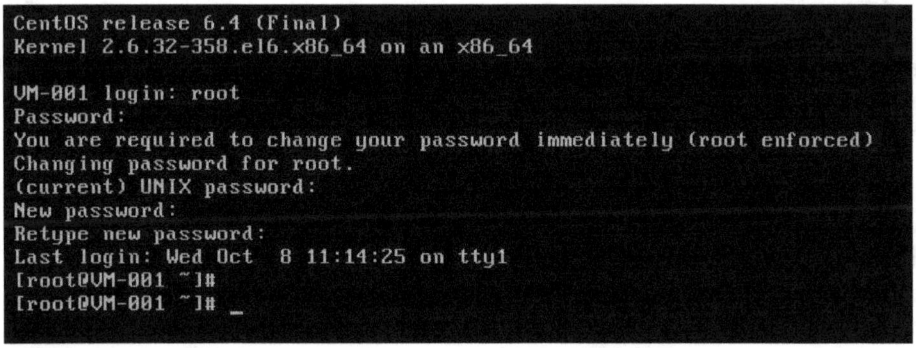

```
CentOS release 6.4 (Final)
Kernel 2.6.32-358.el6.x86_64 on an x86_64

VM-001 login: root
Password:
You are required to change your password immediately (root enforced)
Changing password for root.
(current) UNIX password:
New password:
Retype new password:
Last login: Wed Oct  8 11:14:25 on tty1
[root@VM-001 ~]#
[root@VM-001 ~]# _
```

You will be prompted to change this password on your first login. Provide a strong new password that contains at least one special character, and contains an alphanumeric pattern as well.

There you have it! Your very own Linux virtual machine on the cloud!

Monitoring virtual machines

Monitoring your virtual machines' workloads is an equally important and challenging task for any cloud administrator. A good monitoring system can provide the administrators with clear visibility of what is actually happening with their workloads on the cloud. VMware vCloud Air offers a simple insight into your cloud environment by providing basic graphs for monitoring your virtual machine's performances and workloads.

These graphs can be accessed by selecting your virtual machine name from the dashboard, and then selecting the **Monitoring Tab** as shown here:

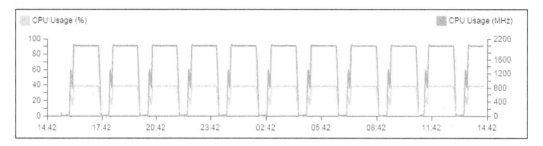

Here, you can view and compare **CPU**, **Memory**, and **Disk performances** of your virtual machine for an hour, a day, and even a month. This helps you analyze and improve your virtual machine's performance over a period of time.

 Hovering over the graph will also display the metric values of that particular interval of time.

For administrators who wish to have a more in-depth view and control of their cloud infrastructure, they can also integrate VMware's **vRealize Operations Manager** with vCloud Air.

You can have a vRealize Operations Manager instance running on an on-premise VMware vSphere or a vCloud Director infrastructure, managing and monitoring local servers and applications. At the same time, leverage **vCenter Hyperic** to collect server and application-related data from both the on-premise and vCloud Air infrastructure. These performance metrics and data are then relayed back to the vRealize Operations manager where they can be analyzed. They provide the administrators with a consolidated view of both on-premises and cloud workloads. We will be exploring more about vRealize Operations Manager and its uses later in *Chapter 5, Monitoring Workloads on vCloud Air*.

Best practices and tips

Here are some of the best useful practices and tips that you should keep in mind when working with virtual machines in vCloud Air:

1. Use role-based access and authorization mechanisms wherever you can. This ensures that only the right people have the required administrative and access rights to create and work with the virtual machines.

2. Monitor virtual machines for performance. Use tools to gauge your infrastructure consumptions and then dial down or increase resources as required. This prevents unnecessary usage of resources and also stops VM sprawls.

3. Use proper backup solutions to perform backups of your virtual machines. Snapshotting is not a good backup solution and should be avoided as a backup utility at all times.

4. Remember to power off your virtual machines when not in use to avoid incurring unnecessary costs.

5. Always install **VMware Tools** on your virtual machines. By default, all templates created under the vCloud Air catalog have VMware Tools preinstalled on them. You will need to perform this activity for the virtual machines that you create from scratch.

6. Design for failure and nothing will fail. Use regions to host your applications, and virtual machines in different geographically isolated datacenters. Remember, a public cloud too can fail, but it is always your responsibility to make sure that your application doesn't.

Summary

Let's have a quick recap of the things that we have covered in this chapter so far.

First off, we looked at what exactly virtual machines, vApps, templates, and catalogs are. We then went through some simple ways by which you can create your very own virtual machines on the vCloud Air platform. We also learned some of the operational steps that can be performed on virtual machines, such as power operations, editing the virtual machine's properties using both the vCloud Air and the vCloud Director portal, and more. We also saw how to import readymade templates and vApps into our vCloud Air catalogs using the Solutions Exchange site. And last but not least, we learned about a few good practices and tips that one should always bear in mind when designing, building, and working with virtual machines.

In the next chapter, we will have a look at some of the networking concepts, options, and services provided by vCloud Air.

3
vCloud Air Networking and Security

In *Chapter 2*, *Working with Virtual Machines*, we explored the concepts of templates, vApps, and virtual machines. We also explored some easy ways to create, edit, and manage virtual machines, along with some best key practices and tips as takeaways. In this chapter, we are going to walk through the following topics:

- An overview of networks and networking concepts in vCloud Air
- Connecting your virtual machines to different networks
- Some key network-related services provided by vCloud Air

The vCloud Air networking components

Networking is a key aspect and function of any cloud provider. A properly designed and implemented network in a cloud is essential for better performance and the security of your overall infrastructure.

VMware vCloud Air provides the same level of networking technologies and services that you would find in a traditional hosting or a datacenter provider; the only minor difference being that most of these services are provided in a software form rather than the conventional hardware. This concept is commonly referred to as **Software Defined Networking,** or **SDN** in short, and VMware leverages it to create and provide software-based networks in vCloud Air.

Apart from the standard VMware vSphere and vCloud Director software, the following VMware products and solutions work together to provide the SDN functionality in vCloud Air:

- VXLAN: a VXLAN, or **Virtual eXtensible Local Area Network,** is a part of the vCloud Networking and Security product suite. It provides the necessary functionality to create and manage scalable virtual networks in a cloud environment by overlaying virtualized layer 2 networks over layer 3 networks.

  By using a VXLAN, you can provision a virtual machine that can communicate with another virtual machine, residing on a different network without having to configure physical switches and routers, thus saving time and reducing overall complexities for the end users.

- VMware vShield Edge: VMware **vShield Edge** is also a part of the vCloud Networking and Security product suite. It basically functions as an edge network device that can provide essential network and security services to virtual datacenters (VDCs), such as the ones used in vCloud Air.

  vShield Edge has integration capabilities with the VMware vSphere and vCloud environments, and provides the following features and services to each of them:

  - A stateful firewall that controls both inbound and outbound network traffic
  - A network address translation to and from the vCloud Air environment
  - A DHCP service for providing IP addresses to virtual machines dynamically
  - Virtual load balancers for balancing web traffic
  - A site-to-site VPN that enables you to connect your in-house datacenters to vCloud Air

We will be exploring each of these services in detail later on in this chapter.

Gateways and networks

When you log in to the vCloud Air dashboard, you can select any of your existing virtual datacenters and view the details about its default gateway and networks. But what are these gateways and networks, and how are they useful to us?

Gateways

In vCloud Air, gateways are nothing more than the VMware vShield Edge devices that we talked about earlier. Each VDC comes with its own gateway.

When you subscribe to a Virtual Private Cloud service, VMware creates your virtual datacenter for you and adds a default gateway to that virtual datacenter. When you subscribe to a Dedicated Cloud service, then you, as an end user, have to log in to the vCloud Air dashboard and create your first virtual datacenter. When you allocate a public IP address to your virtual datacenter, vCloud Air automatically creates a gateway in that virtual datacenter.

 Note that you can create multiple gateways using the **vCloud Air Dedicated Cloud** service. However, a virtual datacenter created inside a **Virtual Private Cloud** service has only a single gateway attached to it.

Gateways are responsible for providing external connectivity to your virtual machines, which are hosted on the vCloud Air platform. They provide other networking services such as DHCP, NAT, load balancing, static routing, and site-to-site VPN connectivity as well.

A gateway has the following properties:

- A gateway, by default, comprises minimal footprint and resource utilization
- HA (high availability) is enabled
- An external network IP that connects directly to the Internet
- An internal network range with an IP range and subnet

A gateway consists of ten network interfaces. One of these interfaces is used for the external world connectivity. You can configure various network segments on the remaining nine interfaces according to your requirements.

You can view the gateway configuration by selecting the virtual datacenter and the **Gateways** tab, as shown below. You can manage the granular aspects of the gateway by selecting the **Manage in vCloud Director** option, as follows:

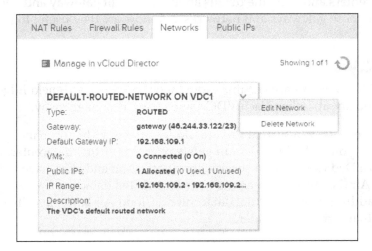

Networks

When you first subscribe to vCloud Air and a default VDC is created, two types of networks are also populated in it by default. These networks have their own set of IP ranges and subnets, and can be used in different situations as required.

These networks are called routed and isolated networks, respectively.

The default-routed network is a gateway-based network, and connects directly to the edge gateway. As a result, virtual machines created on this network can have Internet-facing capabilities in them. The other network is called as a default-isolated network, and this is not connected to the Edge gateway device. As a result, all virtual machines created here remain isolated from the external world.

A combination of both the routed and isolated networks can be used to create DMZ-like zones within your VDC, which can allow only a particular set of virtual machines to interface with the Internet, while the rest remain isolated and secured on isolated networks. Here is a look at a simple DMZ zone created using a combination of gateways and networks:

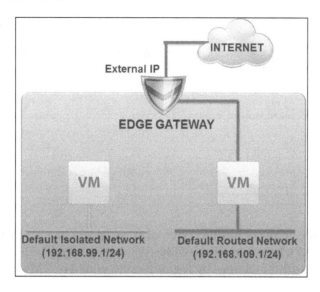

Let's have a quick look at what the default setup is for each network:

Settings	Routed networks	Isolated networks
Default name:	DATACENTER_NAME-DEFAULT-ROUTED	DATACENTER_NAME-DEFAULT-ISOLATED
Internet connectivity:	Yes	No
Default IP Range:	• IP Range: 192.168.109.2-192.168.109.254 • Subnet: 255.255.255.0	• IP Range: 192.168.99.2-192.168.99.254 • Subnet: 255.255.255.0
Services provided:	DHCP, NAT, Firewall, load balancing, SSL VPN, static routing	Only DHCP

To view the network configurations, select the VDC from the vCloud Air dashboard, and then select the Networks tab, as shown here:

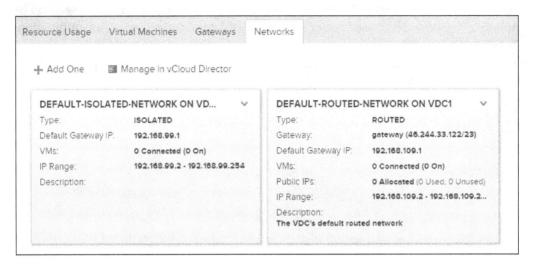

In this example, the gateway has the external IP **46.244.33.122**. VMware vCloud Air's Virtual Private Cloud service provides you two public IP addresses by default. You can purchase additional ones by logging on to your My VMware account and subscribing to them.

> **IMPORTANT**: Virtual machines that are connected to the routed network do not get any Internet access by default. You have to configure both firewall and NAT rules to allow your virtual machine to communicate with the outside world. By default, the gateway has firewall set to deny all traffic to and from the virtual machine, on the gateway networks.

You can edit the network address ranges in both the routed and isolated networks by simply selecting the Edit Network option, provided on each network's drop-down option. In this case, we have edited the default-routed network of our VDC, and we have set a new IP range (**192.168.109.2 - 192.168.109.100**).

You can even add more network segments here by selecting the + sign next to the **IP Range** field. Once done, select the **Edit Network** option to save the changes that you just made.

Your new network configurations may take a few seconds to be applied. Once done, you can verify the change by viewing the **Network** tab as done earlier.

Assigning the public IPs

Now that we have understood the concepts of the gateway and networks, let's look at how easily you can assign public IP addresses using VMware vCloud Air.

When you first subscribe to vCloud Air, you will be provided with a few public IP addresses as a part of your service offering. You can purchase additional public IP addresses as needed using the **Subscription Services** in My VMware portal.

By default, you will be provided with two public IP addresses when you sign up for a Virtual Private Cloud service.

Note that you should allocate public IP addresses to your virtual machines only when you want them to be connected to the Internet.

Each time you allocate a public IP address, you are actually allocating to the gateway's external interface. To get started, select the **Gateways** tab on your main dashboard. Next, select the **Gateway** instance itself to bring up the following screen:

Select the Public IPs tab and select the Add IP Address option to get started. It is important to remember that assigning public IP addresses incurs additional charges, so make sure you add one only when required. Once added, you can view your public IP address from the same tab that you are currently in, as follows:

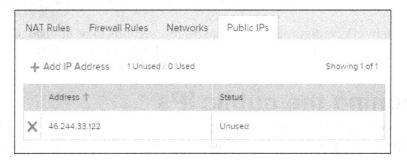

In this case, the public IP assigned to the gateway's external interface is **46.244.33.122**. Note that the status of the IP address shows that it is currently unused. This is because we have not assigned it to a virtual machine as of yet.

Connecting virtual machines to a network

You can connect your virtual machines to both the routed and isolated networks using a variety of methods, the simplest one being selecting the correct network type during the virtual machine's creation phase. You can optionally modify the network parameters using the vCloud Director console as well, but for this scenario, we will be using the vCloud Air interface to do so.

> Note that when you connect a virtual machine to a network, it will be assigned a specific IP from that network's private IP range. For example, a routed network will provide the virtual machine an IP in the range of 192.168.109.2 - 192.168.109.254.

To connect your virtual machine to a specific network, follow the following steps:

1. Select the virtual machine's **Name** from the Virtual Machines dashboard.

If your virtual machine is in a power-on state, then select it first and power it off using the **Actions** tab.

1. Click on the **Networks** tab of your virtual machine.

2. Click on the **Add a Network** option, as shown next. This will pop up a list of networks existing in your VDC, namely the routed and isolated network. Select the network of your choice and hit **Save** when done, as shown:

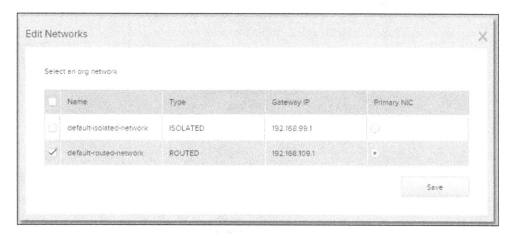

You can select one or more networks for your virtual machine; however, you do need to specify the virtual machine's Primary NIC option for that network. The virtual machine always accepts the first NIC attached to it as the primary interface.

Connecting virtual machines to the Internet

With your virtual machines all set with their networks, you can now connect them to the external world using these simple steps for the scenarios shown:

 IMPORTANT: Make sure that your virtual machine is connected to the routed network and in a powered-on state. Also, make sure you have assigned a public IP address to the gateway as we did earlier in this chapter.

Scenario

We have a production Web Server called as PROD-HTTP-1, deployed on the vCloud Air portal. This is a CentOS 6.5 64 bit vanilla virtual machine connected to the default-routed network as shown below. We need to connect this virtual machine to the Internet so that:

- We can install the necessary Apache Web Server packages (httpd)
- We can connect and view the Web Server from our local desktops using the Internet as shown:

To get started, we first need to add a couple of NAT rules and open up the firewall ports on the gateway, so that our virtual machine can connect to the internet.

From the Gateways tab, select the **default gateway** icon option to view its associated NAT and Firewall rules. By default, NAT is disabled and the firewall is set to deny all traffic to and from the virtual machines on the routed network.

In the **NAT** tab, select the **Add a NAT Rule** option to create your first NAT rule. There are two types of NAT rules that you can specify using the vCloud Air console:

- SNAT: **Source NAT** (SNAT) is configured when the traffic is moving from the virtual machine hosted in vCloud Air to the internet, through the external network

- DNAT: **Destination NAT** (DNAT) is configured when the traffic is moving from the internet to a virtual machine, hosted inside the vCloud Air environment

In our example, the first NAT that we are configure is the SNAT, which will allow our virtual machine to connect to the internet.

Select the **SNAT** option in the **Type** field and provide the virtual machine's IP address in the Original (Internal) Source field, and the gateway's public IP address in the Translated (External) Source field. Remember to select the option to **Enable this rule** as well before you click on the **Next** button, as shown:

The next dialog box will show you the SNAT rule you just created, along with an additional option to add more NAT rules, so before closing this wizard, let's add one DNAT rule as well. Click on **Add** to add a new NAT rule.

This time, select the **DNAT** option from the Type field. As you can see, there are a lot more fields to fill up here, so let's take it one at a time.

In the **Original (External) IP** field, enter the gateway's public IP address that we configured earlier in this chapter. Now, according to our scenario, we want our Web Server to be accessible on the internet. For this, we will **NAT** all the traffic flowing on the virtual machine's internal port 80 (the default port for web traffic) to the gateway's external port (here, we have used 80 for that as well). Once you have filled out all the required details as shown below, click on **Next** to continue.

You will see your two NAT rules as shown here. Once you have reviewed the settings, click on **Finish** to create these NAT rules.

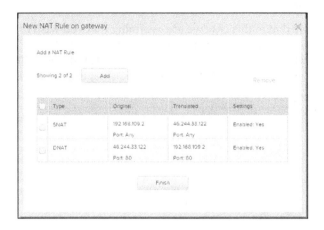

The two NAT rules will appear on your vCloud Air dashboard as shown below. You can further choose the enable/disable NAT rules, or edit them by selecting each individual NAT rule using the checkbox provided alongside it and selecting the **Actions** tab to select what particular action you wish to perform on them.

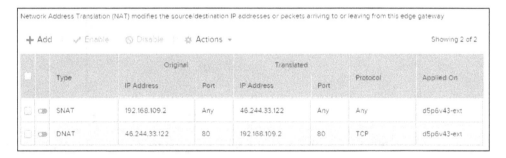

Once the NAT rules are in place, we have to open up the necessary ports on the firewall as well to allow the traffic to pass through. To do so, simply select the **Firewall** tab and select the **Add Firewall Rule** option to get started. Like the NAT rules, we will be creating two firewall rules for our virtual machine as well. The first rule will enable the Internet connectivity to the virtual machine.

To do this, first provide a suitable **Name** to the firewall rule; in this case, we have called it as `Internet`. You can choose to enable this rule and **Log network traffic** for this exception. For this rule, we have selected both these options.

Next, provide the values for the **Protocol, Source** and **Destination** fields as shown here.

> Note that in this case we are assuming that you wish to allow any traffic from the **Source** (Internal virtual machine IP) to the **Destination** (the Internet). You can create additional, fine-grained firewall rules for Internet access according to your requirements.

Once done, click on **Next** to continue. In the **Summary** page, click on the **Add** button to add an additional firewall rule. This rule will allow access to the Web Server's default port 80 on the firewall, so that we can access the same over the Internet.

Provide a suitable **Name** for the new firewall rule; in this case, we have called it `Port 80`. Make sure you select the **Enable** option for this rule as well.

For this rule, we want a very specific port to be opened up on a very specific range. So, fill up the details in the fields as shown here:

- **Source field**: This is the specific CIDR, IP, or IP range. This provides the internal IP address of the virtual machine.

- **Source Port**: This provides the web server's default port. Here, that is 80.

- **Destination field**: This is the specific CIDR, IP, or IP range. This provides the public IP address of the gateway.
- **Destination Port**: We have opted to go with port 80 on the destination side as well. You can provide a different port value here for an added measure of security.

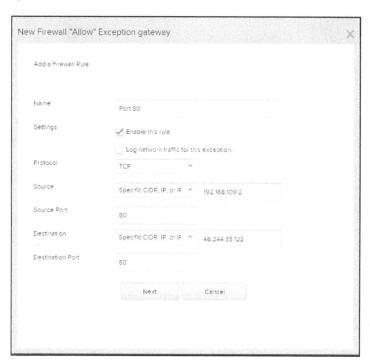

The Add a Firewall Rule tab

Once you are happy with the settings, click on **Next** to proceed and **Finish** the firewall additions. You will see your firewall rules added in the **Firewalls** tab as shown next.

You can further choose the enable/disable firewall rules, or even edit them, by selecting each individual rule using the checkbox provided alongside it. Select the **Actions** tab to select a particular action that you wish to perform on them, as shown here:

With all the configurations completed, log in to the virtual machine using the VMRC, and test the following scenarios out:

1. Type the following command and check whether you are able to download the `httpd` packages:

    ```
    # yum install httpd
    ```

    Once the packages are downloaded, start the Apache Web Server using the following command:

    ```
    # service httpd start
    ```

2. From your local desktop, open up a browser and type in the public IP address. You will see the **Apache 2 Test Page** as shown here:

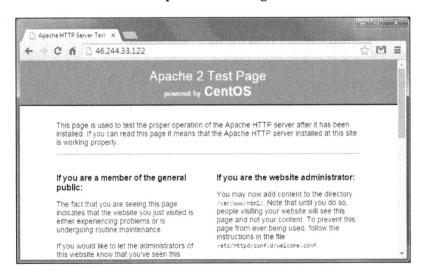

In this way, you can configure and use similar NAT and firewalls rules for any virtual machine that you wish to connect to the Internet.

Networking services provided by gateways

In the beginning of this chapter, we explored the basic function and capabilities of gateways and networks. In this section, we will be looking at some of the core network services that are provided by gateways, and see how these services can be leveraged in different scenarios.

There are two ways to go about managing gateways: You can perform the basic functions well using the vCloud Air console, but when it comes to the networking services, you should manage the gateways using the VMware vCloud Director interface. Let's quickly see how to manage and work with the gateway using VMware vCloud Director's console.

From the main dashboard, select your Virtual Datacenter. Next, from the **Gateways** tab, select the **Manage in vCloud Director** option as shown here:

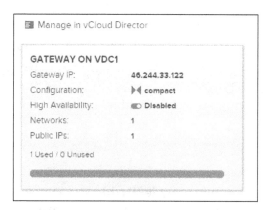

Using single sign-in, this should automatically log you into the vCloud Director interface. From here, we can effectively create, edit, and manage all aspects of our vCloud Air platform, including gateways, networks, vApps, catalogs, and even custom templates.

If you do not see the VDC's gateway on your screen, then use these directions to view the gateway. From the vCloud Director interface, select the **Administration** tab. In the Administration pane to the left, select **Virtual Datacenters**. You will see a list of all the virtual datacenters currently in use. Select any one of them to get started with.

Once the VDC is selected, from the right-hand pane, select the **Edge Gateways** tab as shown below. This will bring up default gateway and associated network services.

You can right-click on the gateway's name to view its **Properties**, as shown here:

Here, you can view the gateway's default settings, such as whether it is configured in High Availability mode or not, what external IP networks are configured on the gateway, IP pools information, and more. Once you have browsed through the properties, exit the dialog box and return to the **Edge Gateways** tab.

To view the different services offered by gateways, right-click on the gateway's name once again, and select the **Edge Gateway Services** option. This will bring up a dialog box that will help you configure each individual network service, which we will discuss in depth now.

DHCP

The DHCP service allows you to provide IP addresses to your virtual machines automatically when they boot up. By default, this service is disabled in gateways, so you will need to enable it first in order for it to work. To enable the DHCP service, simply check the checkbox called **Enable DHCP**.

Note that the DHCP service is available for both routed and
isolated networks. You can configure DHCP for an isolated
network using the vCloud Director interface by going to the
Administration page | **Virtual Datacenters** | **org VDC Networks**
tab. Here, right-click on the default-isolated network and select the
Configure Services option.

To create a DHCP network segment on the routed network, simply click on the **Add**
button as shown here:

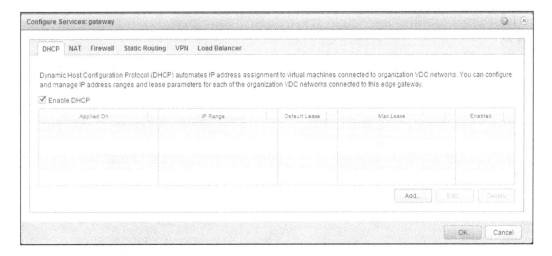

You can create multiple pools of DHCP servers, each with its own set of
DHCP IP address ranges. In this example, we have configured an IP range of
192.168.109.110 - 192.168.109.120 for our routed network. You can optionally
change the **Default lease time** (3600 seconds = 1 hour), and the **Max lease time**
(7200 seconds = 2 hours), according to your requirements, as shown here:

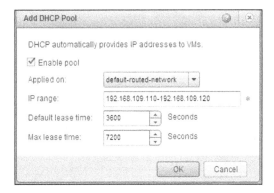

Once configured, select **OK**. You will see your DHCP pool added and ready for use. Before you check on the virtual machine, it is important to close the **Configure Services** dialog box by clicking on **OK**, as the gateway will then reload itself and apply the changed configuration settings to the network as well.

To provide a virtual machine with a DHCP-based IP address, select the **Home** tab. Click on **Manage vApps**. Here, select the vApp that you wish to edit. Make sure the vApp is powered off before you proceed. Right-click on the virtual machine's name and select **Properties**. In the **Hardware** tab, you can change the IP mode setting from **Static – IP Pool** to **DHCP**.

NAT

As we saw earlier with the vCloud Air UI, we can configure network address translation using the vCloud Director's gateway services as well.

Right-click on the gateway's name and select **Edge Gateway Services**. Select the **NAT** tab as shown below. You will already see a couple of NAT rules added here. These were added by vCloud Air during our Web Server use case scenario, earlier in this chapter. The principles remain the same; you can add SNAT and DNAT rules using this dialog box according to your requirements.

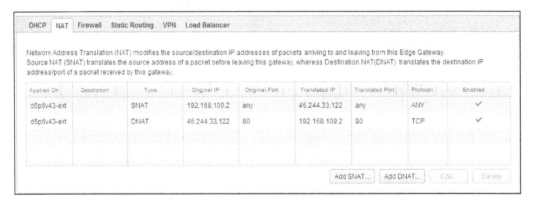

Applied On	Description	Type	Original IP	Original Port	Translated IP	Translated Port	Protocol	Enabled
d5p6v43-ext		SNAT	192.168.109.2	any	46.244.33.122	any	ANY	✓
d5p6v43-ext		DNAT	46.244.33.122	80	192.168.109.2	80	TCP	✓

In this example, let us quickly create a DNAT rule that will allow us to access our Web Server (PROD-HTTP-1 virtual machine) over SSH from our local desktops. Select the **Add DNAT** option. This will pop up the following wizard that will help you create a DNAT rule:

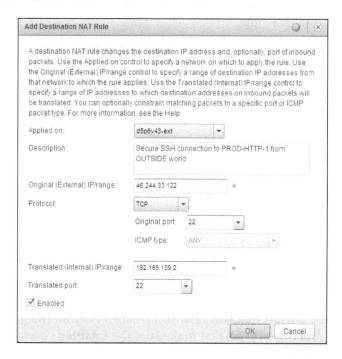

In the **Original (External) IP/range** field, provide the public IP address of the gateway. Select **TCP** as **Protocol** and provide destination port as 22 (default for SSH). In the **Translated (Internal) IP/range** field, provide the internal IP address of the PROD-HTTP-1 virtual machine along with the **Translated port**, which also happens to be TCP port 22.

Once done, make sure to check the **Enabled** checkbox. Click on **OK** to save the settings. You are almost ready to access your virtual machine, but wait! You have to open up the required port on the firewall as well. So, next up in the networking services is the firewall.

The Firewall

Just as with NAT, you can manage the firewall settings using both the vCloud Air and vCloud Director as well. You will see two firewall rules already created here; one for allowing internet traffic, and the other to allow traffic on **Port 80** of the PROD-HTTP-1 virtual machine.

To add a new firewall rule, simply click on the **Add** option, as shown here:

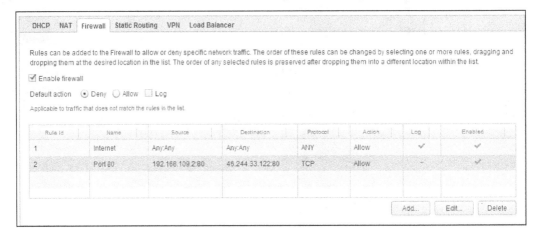

This will bring up a wizard that will help you create a firewall rule to allow inbound access on port 22 (SSH). To do so, first make sure the **Enabled** checkbox is checked. Next, provide a suitable Name for your firewall rule; in this case, we have called it SECURE22.

Provide the virtual machine's internal IP address in the **Source** field, and select 22 from the **Source port** drop-down list.

Similarly, provide the public IP address of the gateway in the **Destination** field followed by the **Destination port 22**. You can optionally log network traffic for this particular firewall rule if required. Once done, click on OK to save the rule.

Next up, from your local desktop, open up a Putty session and pass the public IP address of the gateway with port 22 in it.

You will be able to connect to the PROD-HTTP-1 virtual machine as shown here:

Static routing

Most network routing is done dynamically where the router automatically chooses the best path between two network endpoints. A static route is a preprogrammed path between two networks and is mainly used in place of the dynamic routing for security reasons.

You can create two types of static routes using vCloud Director:

- From one vApp network to another vApp network in the same organization
- From one vApp network to another vApp network in a different organization

When do you use static routing? Let's look at the following examples and understand a bit more about static routing:

- Case 1: You have a web server inside a vApp running in one VDC. The VDC passes traffic to the outside world using the public IP address as we have seen earlier in this chapter. We also have another application server running on a vApp in a different VDC altogether. This VDC too connects to the Internet using a public IP address. Now, you wish these two vApps to communicate with each other, but you don't want the traffic to pass through the Internet. In this case, a static route will be a perfect solution to the problem. You can create a static route between the two VDC gateways, and force the traffic between the vApps through it, thus shielding your vApps from the Internet and providing additional security as well.

- Case 2: You want any and all incoming traffic from the Internet to pass through a software-based firewall, or some anti-virus appliance, before it reaches your virtual machines. In this case, too, a static route can prove to be useful.

To enable a static route in vCloud Director, right-click on the gateway's name and select **Edge Gateway Services**. Select the **Static Routing** tab. This will bring up the following dialog box that will help you create a static route between the two networks:

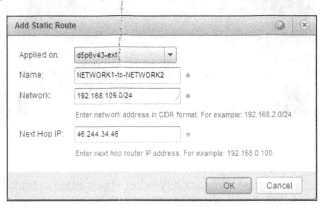

Next, follow the given steps:

1. Fill in the required information according to your requirements.
2. Select the network interface through which the traffic will be routed.
3. Next, provide a suitable **Name** for the static route.
4. In the **Network** field, provide a network address in CIDR format. The network address field is for the first vApp network to which you want to add a static route.
5. In the **Next Hop IP** field, provide the external IP address of that vApp network's gateway router.
6. Once done, click on OK to save the configurations. Remember to select the **Enable static routing** checkbox before you close the **Configuring Services** dialog box for the gateway.

 It is important to *note* that, although you have created and established a static route between the two networks, you still need to allow traffic between them using the firewall rules.

Virtual private networks

VMware vCloud Air provides you with the ability to connect your on-premise datacenters with vCloud Air in a variety of ways, such as the Internet, secure VPNs, and Direct Connect.

 Direct Connect is a network offering provided by vCloud Air that helps you connect your on-premise datacenter with vCloud Air using a dedicated, high-speed, low-latency network. You can read more about it here: `http://vcloud.vmware.com/service-offering/direct-connect`

Enabling a VPN in vCloud Director provides you with the following connectivity options:

- VPN tunnels between two organization networks in the same organization
- VPN tunnels between two organization networks in two different organizations
- VPN tunnels between an organization network and a remote network outside of VMware vCloud

We will be exploring more on VPNs and site-to-site connectivity options later on in *Chapter 5, Monitoring Workloads on vCloud Air*.

Load balancing

A very interesting and useful service and feature provided by the gateway is that of load balancing. You can leverage the gateway as a ready-to-use load balancer for your applications, just as you would use a standard hardware-based load balancer or some open source load balancing software, such as **HAProxy**.

Let's explore this load balancing feature with a use-case scenario:

Scenario

We have two productions: Web Servers called `PROD-HTTP-1` and `PROD-HTTP-2` deployed on the vCloud Air portal. These are CentOS 6.5 64 bit vanilla virtual machines connected to the default-routed network as shown next. Both the virtual machines have a web server (Apache `httpd` packages) installed and configured in them. Our main goal is to leverage the gateway as a load balancer for these two web servers.

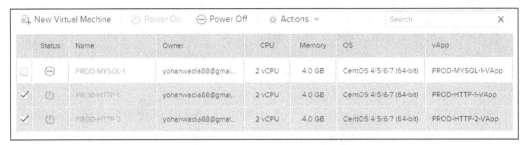

Two Web Servers deployed on vCloud Air

Each web server has a simple `index.html` file created within the `/var/www/html` directory structure. A snippet of the file created for PROD-HTTP-1 virtual machine is shown here:

```
<html>
<body bgcolor="black"><font color="white">
<center><h1>This is HTTP PROD SERVER 1</h1></center>
</font></body>
</html>
```

For the PROD-HTTP-2 virtual machine, we have used the same file contents by just replacing the background color with red, and the text with "This is HTTP PROD SERVER 2", so that we can distinguish both the servers and check whether load balancing is actually taking place or not.

To get started, first right-click on the gateway and select the **Edge Gateway Services** option. Next, select the **Load Balancer** tab. Here, you will find two sub tabs, namely **Pool Servers** and **Virtual Servers**:

- **Pool Servers**: This is basically a container that will contain all the servers that you wish to load balance. Alternatively, you can also specify which protocol you wish to load balance over using this section.

Virtual Servers: As the name suggests, these are virtual servers that actually sit at the top of the pool servers and act as load balancers. You can assign each virtual server a VIP (virtual IP), and also select the protocols that you wish to enable for load balancing.

The Pool Servers and Virtual Servers setting under Edge Gateway Services

Click on the Add button. This will bring up the **Add Load Balancer Member Pool** wizard. The first screen will prompt you to provide a **Name** and an optional Description for your pool servers. In this case, we have named our pool servers HTTP-PROD-SERVERS. Click on **Next** to continue.

In the **Configure Service** page, shown as follows, select the **Service** and **Load Balancing Method** of your choice. For this scenario, we have gone ahead and selected the **HTTP** service and **Round Robin** as the load balancing method.

VMware supports **IP Hash**, **Least Connections**, **Round Robin**, and **URI** as the balancing algorithms, of which **Round Robin** is the simplest to use. Once done, click on Next to proceed with the configuration.

In the next **Configure Health-Checks** page, it checks for your pool servers.

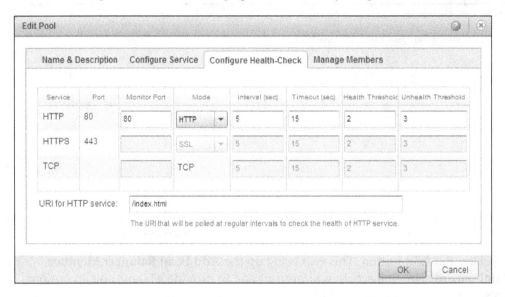

The **Health-Check** option checks that all the servers in the pool are alive and are answering queries. The following parameters can be updated according to your requirements. We have gone ahead and stuck with the default values:

- **Interval**: This is the interval in seconds at which a server is pinged
- **Timeout**: The time in seconds within which a response from the server must be received
- **Health Threshold**: The number of successful and consecutive health checks before a server is declared operational
- **Unhealth Threshold**: The number of consecutive unsuccessful health checks before a server is declared dead

In the next page, click on the **Add** button to add the two web server virtual machines that we have created.

 Note that both the virtual machines are powered on and connected to the default-routed network.

In the **Add Member** popup box, provide the IP address value of the PROD-HTTP-1 virtual machine. Type in the default port value of 80 in both the **Port** fields. Repeat the same steps to add the PROD-HTTP-2 virtual machine as well.

The Add Member pop-up box

Verify the pool server settings and configuration, and click on **Finish** when done. With this complete, your pool server is created. Now we need to create the virtual server that will act as the load balancer for our pool server. To do so, select the **Virtual Servers** tab and click on the **Add** button, as shown:

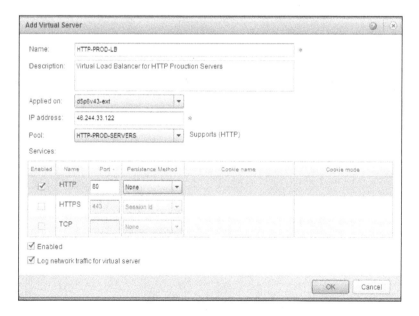

Provide a unique and meaningful **Name** and **Description** for the virtual server. Select the external interface of the gateway in the **Applied on** field. Next, provide the public IP address of the gateway. This is the same IP address that we created some time back in this chapter. You can alternatively create and provide a different public IP here as well.

This IP address will be used as the VIP to load balance the pool servers.

From the **Pool** drop-down, select the recently created pool servers that we created.

Select the HTTP service option and provide the default port **80** value as shown. This is the port on which the web servers will be load balanced. Remember to check the **Enabled** option to enable the virtual server once it's created. You can optionally choose to **Log** network traffic for the virtual server as well. Once done, click on **OK** to complete the procedure.

Give the Edge Gateway approximately 30 seconds to reconfigure. Once completed, you can go ahead and create the necessary firewall and NAT rules to allow traffic flow from the two web servers to the gateway.

First up is the firewall. Open port 80 on the internal IP addresses of the two web servers. The gateway's public IP address will be the destination IP as shown:

	Name	Source	Destination	Protocol	Log
	Internet	Any : Any	Any : Any	Any	Enabled
	Port 80	192.168.109.2 : 80	46.244.33.122 : 80	TCP	Disabled
	SECURE22	192.168.99.2 : 22	192.168.109.2 : 22	TCP	Disabled
	Port 80	192.168.109.3 : 80	46.244.33.122 : 80	TCP	Disabled

Second, we enable DNAT as well, so that both the web servers can be accessed via the gateway's public IP from our local desktops. In this case, the Web Servers internal IP address will be the source IP, and the gateway's public IP address will be the translated IP address as shown:

		Original		Translated			
	Type	IP Address	Port	IP Address	Port	Protocol	Applied On
	SNAT	192.168.109.2	Any	46.244.33.122	Any	Any	d5p6v43-ext
	DNAT	46.244.33.122	80	192.168.109.2	80	TCP	d5p6v43-ext
	DNAT	46.244.33.122	22	192.168.109.2	22	TCP	d5p6v43-ext
	SNAT	192.168.109.3	Any	46.244.33.122	Any	Any	d5p6v43-ext
	DNAT	46.244.33.122	80	192.168.109.3	80	TCP	d5p6v43-ext

To test the load balancer, simply direct your local browser to the following IP address: `http://<PUBLIC_IP_ADDR_OF_GATEWAY>:80/index.html`.

Refresh your browser multiple times to simulate load on the servers. If your settings are correct, you will see the `index.html` page refresh with different background colors.

Best practices and tips

Here are some useful best practices and tips that you should keep in mind when working with networks in vCloud Air:

1. Open only the required ports on the firewall at all times for any virtual machine. Avoid opening all ports unless absolutely necessary.

2. Use the NAT rules carefully. Provide a dedicated network IP address for the Internet and translate only the required internal IP addresses to it.

3. It is good practice to provide differently translated external port numbers for each internal port number when using NAT. For example, if an internal port 22 has to be NATed to an external port, it is always better to provide a larger, more random port number, such as 2323 rather than the default 22.

4. Assign the network administrative rights only to those users who will be creating and modifying the network parameters of your organization. The rest of the users can have read-only privileges as well.

5. Implement a good antivirus solution/product and place all your virtual machines behind it. Make sure the virtual machines are always patched with the latest updates and firmware at all times.

Summary

In this chapter, we have seen how to connect your virtual machines to the Internet securely using the firewall and NAT rules. We also learned the uses of gateways and networks, and how you can leverage them in your own VDCs. Last but not the least, we explored some of the useful networking services provided by vCloud Air, such as DHCP, NAT, firewall, and load balancing. We also covered a few useful best practices and tips that you should keep in mind when working with networks on vCloud Air.

In the next chapter, we will be going a step further with vCloud Air, and exploring some of the different ways in which you can extend your vCloud Air environment with other public and private clouds.

4
Extending vCloud Air

In the previous chapter, *Chapter 3, vCloud Air Networking and Security*, we learned and explored a few simple and easy-to-use networking services provided by VMware vCloud Air. We also examined how to prove our instances in vCloud Air with networks and connect them with the outside world.

In this chapter, we'll dive a bit deeper into the networking arena by visiting the VPN service provided by vCloud Air. Besides this, we will also look at a few different ways in which you will be able to extend your on-premise VMware vSphere and/or VMware vCloud environments to vCloud Air using a tool called VMware vCloud Connector.

VPNs

We briefly discussed VPN back in *Chapter 3, vCloud Air Networking and Security*. In this section, we will explore the VPN functionality in more detail (that is, elaborate VPN once).

VPNs are a crucial networking service that enable IT organizations to extend their physical, virtual, and cloud based environments to other off-site datacenters and cloud environments without compromising on security. Using VPNs and IPsec tunnels, IT organizations can now transfer large data over the Internet to remote locations with ease, thus helping in migrating workloads to and from the different environments as required.

VPNs are supported on both ends of a transmission channel by a firewall and/or a special VPN device that restricts any form of data interception from the outside world.

VPNs are created in VMware vCloud Air using the vShield Edge Gateway appliance. Using the Gateway appliance, you can connect to the following networking topologies:

- **Enterprise site to vCloud environment**: Using vShield Edge Gateway, you can connect your on-site enterprise data centers with a vCloud Air using a standard IPsec tunnel. The Enterprise datacenter will require a virtual/physical VPN appliance from either **Cisco** or **Juniper** to connect to a gateway on the vCloud Air premise.

- **Multi-site vCloud environments**: The vShield Edge Gateway VPNs can be used to connect different VMware-based cloud environments with each other as well. For example, you can connect an on-premise VMware vCloud Director with vCloud Air using a secure VPN IPsec tunnel, thus creating a Hybrid Cloud; or you can even connect two VMware-based public Clouds with each other, such as vCloud Air and BlueLock, or **StratoGen Cloud**.

- **Single-site vCloud Environment**: A vCloud Air environment can contain one or more VDCs, each VDC having its own network subnet and Edge Gateway. Since the underlying network is hosted on the shared infrastructure, these VDCs can be connected securely using vShield Edge VPNs.

Let's have a look at how easily we can create a VPN tunnel between VDCs hosted on the same vCloud Air environment and also between two different VMware Public Clouds.

Site-to-site VPN connectivity

Consider the scenario: We have a PRODUCTION VDC running on a 192.168.109.0/24 subnet, and a DEVELOPMENT VDC running on a 192.168.110.0/24 subnet. We wish to enable a secure VPN between these two VDCs using the VMware vShield Edge Gateway service.

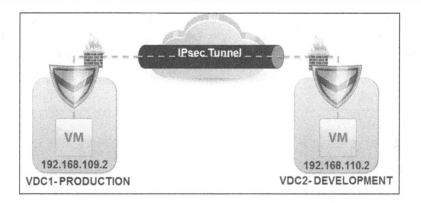

Prerequisites to creating VPN between networks in the same organization are as follows:

- Both the networks must be external facing
- Both the networks must have non-overlapping IP subnets
- Both the networks should have a site-to-site VPN enabled

To get started, first, we need to make sure that both the VDCs have their networks routed through a gateway. From the vCloud Air dashboard, select any VDC, click on the Gateways tab, and select the Manage in vCloud Director option, as shown here:

From the vCloud Director UI, select the **ManageVDCs** option from the options bar. Next, select the **Org VDC Networks** tab to display the types of networks currently present for that particular virtual datacenter. Make sure the virtual machine that you wish to communicate to the other VDC is running on the Routed Interface as shown here:

Run the same check on the other virtual datacenter, making sure that there is a routed network present, and that a virtual machine from that VDC is connected to it.

Now, we add the VPN. To do so, from the vCloud Director UI, select the **Edge Gateway** tab from your VDC. Right-click on the **Edge Gateway** device, and select the **Edge Gateway Services** option:

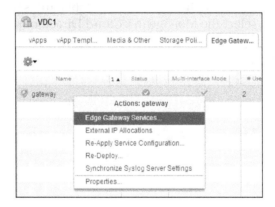

This will bring up the **Gateway's Configure Services** dialog box. Select the **VPN** tab, and click on the **Add** button to get started.

This will bring up the **Add Site-to-Site VPN Configuration** dialog box as shown. Using the wizard, you can create secure VPNs that can connect to the VDCs in the same vCloud Air environment, VDCs across some other vCloud provider such as Bluelock or StratoGen Cloud or even connect to an on premise vSphere environment that's backed up by a vShield Edge Gateway device.

In the **Configure Services** dialog, provide a suitable **Name** for the VPN Tunnel. You can optionally provide Description to go along with it as well. Next, select the **Enable this VPN configuration** checkbox.

As discussed earlier, you can assign a VPN to a network in the current organization or to some other organization, and even connect offsite to a remote network. For this exercise, select the A network in this organization option as shown.

The moment you select this, the local and peer networks field would automatically populate as well. Make sure you select both **Local Networks** and **Peer Networks** before proceeding with the next configuration items.

Once done, you can leave the rest of the VPN configuration parameters to their default values, and click on **OK** to create the VPN tunnel. If all goes well, you will see the VPN details auto-populated on the second VDC's gateway as well:

Next up, enable the firewall rules to allow traffic to and from both the virtual datacenters. To do this, you can use and edit the **Firewall** tab, shown as follows, in the same **Configure Services** dialog, or use the vCloud Air UI to achieve the same. In this case, we have used the vCloud Air UI to allow any traffic coming in from the **PRODUCTION VDC (VDC1)** to the **DEVELOPMENT VDC (VDC2)**.

 Note that opening up all the ports is never a recommended scenario for a production environment. Make sure you open ports that are only required, and add application specific rules when dealing with any production environments.

Save the firewall rules and make sure that the VPN is enabled, and its status shows **OK** on both the gateways before proceeding to the next steps.

 Note that in some cases, the VPN status may show you a **NOT READY** status. This perfectly normal as VPN takes approximately one to two minutes to properly initialize and prep the tunnel for use. So be patient, if you see a **NOT READY** status, check the logs for any issues.

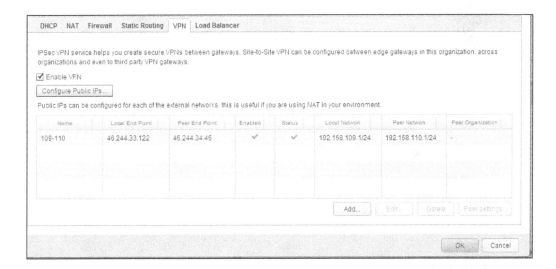

To test VPN to check whether the connectivity was successful or not, simple try to ping the gateway from the PRODUCTION VDC VM to the DEVELOPMENT VDC VM.

Multi-site VPN connectivity

Consider the following scenario: We have a PRODUCTION VDC running on a 192.168.109.0/24 subnet on our VMware vCloud Air environment, and another VDC running on a 198.19.99.0/24 subnet, but on a completely different public cloud called StratoGen Cloud. We wish to enable a secure VPN between these two VDCs using VMware vShield Edge Gateway Service.

Note that StratoGen Cloud provides a wide range of VMware-based Cloud hosting services, such as private cloud, hybrid cloud, and disaster recovery as a service. It runs completely off a VMware vCloud Director environment with major datacenters present in Europe, the United States, and Asia. StratoGen offers a free seven day trial period for its VMware-hosted Cloud. You can read more about it at `http://www.stratogen.net/products/vmware-hosting.html`.

Prerequisites to creating VPN between networks in different organization are as follows:

- Both the networks must be external facing
- Both the networks must have non-overlapping IP subnets
- Both the networks should have a site-to-site VPN enabled

To begin with, first we need to gather some details about our vShield Edge Gateway and running instance at StratoGen Cloud. To do so, log in to the StratoGen Cloud UI, which is a VMware vCloud Director-based self-service portal, and select the **Administration** tab as shown. Select the **Virtual Datacenters** option from under the **Cloud Resources** tab to bring up your VDC. As you can see, the StratoGen VDC also contains two network interfaces, one called **Direct Internet Connection**, which directly connects the instances to the Internet, and the other a **Routed-Network**, which passes all the network traffic from a vShield Edge Gateway device. We will be using the routed network for this connectivity exercise.

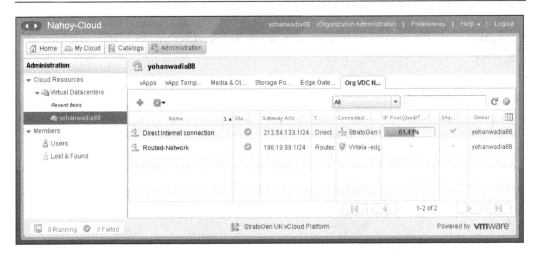

Next, select the **EdgeGateway** tab to view the **Gateway** device. Here, we need to find out the external IP that is provided to the gateway device. This IP is used to pass all the traffic from the VVDC to the Internet. To check the external IP address, right-click on **Gateway** and select the **Properties** option. This will bring up an **Edge Gateway** properties dialog as shown. Select the **Configure IP Settings** tab as shown. Here, make a note of the IP address.

 Note that the external IP address is configured and provided by StratoGen. By default, a single IP address is provided, but you can always contact the StratoGen Support team for more.

Once noted, select **OK** and close this dialog window:

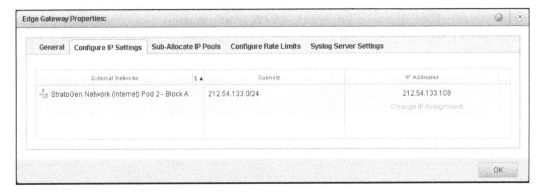

Next, we'll now move over to our vCloud Air environment. This is where we will configure our VPN tunnel to StratoGen Cloud. You can set up the VPN on either of the Clouds as you see fit.

From the vCloud Air UI dashboard, right-click on the VDC name and select the option **Manage** in vCloud Director. This will take you to the vCloud Director UI from where, we will configure the VPN service. Follow the same path as we did with the StratoGen Cloud, that is, select the **Administration** tab | Under the **Virtual Datacenters** option, and select your VDC. Next, select the **Edge Gateway** option, right-click on the **Gateway**, and select the **Edge Gateway Services** option as shown here:

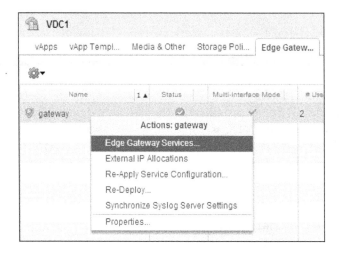

Select the **VPN** tab and click on Add to create a new VPN connection. This will pop up the **Add a Site-to-Site VPN configuration** dialog. Just as before, provide a suitable name for this particular VPN connectivity; in this case, we provided vCloudAir-StratoGen. You can optionally even provide **Description** as required. Select the checkbox that says **Enable this VPN configuration**. Next, from the **Establish VPN** to list, select the `a network in another organization` option as shown here:

IMPORTANT: The vCloud Director UI requires the latest version of Java to be installed on your local machine, as well as Java support for the browser.

You will see an option to Login to Remote VCD as shown here:

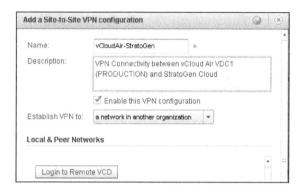

Enter the following information as requested:

- **vCloud URL**: Here, you only need to provide the base URL of your vCloud Director; for example, `http://mycloud.stratogen.net/`. Do not provide `cloud/` or `org/`.

- **Organization**: Here, provide the name of the remote organization that you wish to connect to. In most cases, the organization name is followed after the cloud/org in the vCloud URL.

- **Username/Password**: Here, provide the credentials as supplied by your cloud administrator.

Once all the required fields are filled in, click on **Login** to complete the connectivity. The login takes a few minutes to complete. Once it's done, you will see your StratoGen Cloud's organization VDC and **Peer Edge Gateway** loaded automatically as shown here:

Select the IP subnets provided under the **Local Networks** and **Peer Networks** fields:

- **Local Networks**: This is the network that you wish to designate as the internal network for the VPN (192.168.109.0/24)

- **Peer Networks**: The Peer Network is the remote network for the VPN; in this case, the Routed-Network, from our StratoGen Cloud (198.19.99.0/24)

You can optionally choose to edit VPN connection settings such as **Encryption Protocol**, **Shared Key** and **MTU** size as required. However, in this case we are going to leave them to their default values. Once completed, click on **OK** to finish the VPN configuration.

The VPN tunnel can take up to five to ten minutes to properly establish a secure connection to and from the remote site. A green check mark should appear under the status column on the **Configure Services VPN** tab. Return to the **VPN** tab of your StratoGen Cloud's Gateway, and verify if the same status is present there as well. If both the statuses show green, then you have successfully configured a VPN tunnel between two vCloud organizations running on different networks!

But wait, that's not all. Remember that although a VPN establishes connectivity between two remote networks, you still need to configure the firewalls to allow the traffic to pass through. The firewall rules have to be set up on both of the Gateways to facilitate a two-way communication. You can edit the firewall rules by simply selecting the **Firewall** tab in the Gateway's **Configure Services** dialog and add the required rules.

To allow traffic to flow from vCloud Air to StratoGen Cloud, do as follows:

- **Name**: It provides a suitable name for the firewall rule; in this case, its vCloudAir-StratoGen.

- **Source**: This provides the Source IP subnet of your vCloud Air VDC (192.168.109.0/24). Here, you can optionally provide a single IP address as well.

- **Source port**: Here, we have selected any but you can choose to allow a specific port, such as SSH: 22 or HTTP: 8080, and more.

- **Destination**: This provides the remote network's IP subnet here (198.19.99.0/24).

- **Destination port**: It provides your destination port settings; here, we have chosen any.

- **Protocol**: You can choose between TCP, UDP, ICMP, or any as the protocols.

Optionally, you can even log network traffic for this particular firewall rule. Make sure the rules are enabled by selecting the **Enabled** checkbox. Once completed, select **OK**.

[Note that the firewall rules can be added via the vCloud Air UI as well.]

Follow the same process to allow the traffic to flow from StratoGen Cloud to VMware vCloud Air:

- **Name**: It provides a suitable name for the firewall rule; in this case, its StratoGen-vCloudAir.

- **Source**: This provides the Source IP subnet of your StratoGen Cloud's VDC (198.19.99.0/24). You can optionally provide here a single IP address as well.

- **Source port**: Here, we have selected any but you can choose to allow a specific port only such as SSH: 22 or HTTP: 8080, and so on.

- **Destination**: This provides the vCloud Air VDC's network's IP subnet here (192.168.109.0/24).

- **Destination port**: This provides your destination port settings; here, we have chosen any.

- **Protocol**: You can choose between TCP, UDP, ICMP, or any such, as the protocols.

Optionally, you can even log network traffic for this particular firewall rule. Make sure the rules are enabled by selecting the **Enabled** checkbox. Once completed, select **OK**.

Rule Id	Name	Source	Destination	Protocol	Action	Log	Enabled
1	HTTP-PROD-DB-2	198.19.99.10:80	external:80	TCP	Allow	--	✓
2	SSH-PROD-DB-2	198.19.99.10:22	external:22	TCP	Allow	--	✓
5	StratorGen-vCloud	198.19.99.0/24:Any	192.168.109.0/24:Any	ANY	Allow	--	✓
6	vCloudAir-StratoGe	192.168.109.0/24:Any	198.19.99.0/24:Any	ANY	Allow	--	✓

To test the connectivity, try pinging the instances to each other. If you see a steady stream of packets being transferred, as shown, then congratulation! You have a fully functioning VPN created between your VMware vCloud Air and StratoGen Cloud!

```
                          PROD-LB-1                    ▶ ⏸ ■ 🔄   🔄🔄🔄   ⬛⬛⬛

[root@PROD-LB-1 ~]#
[root@PROD-LB-1 ~]# ping 192.168.109.110
PING 192.168.109.110 (192.168.109.110) 56(84) bytes of data.
64 bytes from 192.168.109.110: icmp_seq=1 ttl=62 time=4.66 ms
64 bytes from 192.168.109.110: icmp_seq=2 ttl=62 time=2.47 ms
64 bytes from 192.168.109.110: icmp_seq=3 ttl=62 time=2.54 ms
64 bytes from 192.168.109.110: icmp_seq=4 ttl=62 time=2.63 ms
^C
--- 192.168.109.110 ping statistics ---
4 packets transmitted, 4 received, 0% packet loss, time 3545ms
rtt min/avg/max/mdev = 2.477/3.079/4.660/0.915 ms
[root@PROD-LB-1 ~]#
[root@PROD-LB-1 ~]# _
```

Extending datacenters to clouds using vCloud Connector

Now that we have seen and used VPNs to simply connect two different vCloud environments, let's explore how you can extend the boundaries of your on-premise datacenters to the public cloud using VMware vCloud Connector.

What is VMware vCloud Connector?

The VMware vCloud Connector is a free tool provided by VMware that helps administrators to create fully functional hybrid cloud environments. Using the vCloud Connector, IT administrators can facilitate orchestration and administration of their on-premise datacenters, as well as a VMware-backed public cloud using a single portal. It is essentially a tool which enables you to migrate your computing resources across vSphere and vCloud environments with ease.

vCloud Connector also enables you to transfer large amounts of data securely from your datacenters to vCloud Air using something called the **Offline Data Transfer (ODT)** service. Using ODT, you can export your data to an external storage device that is provided by a vCloud Air operator, and ship it back to the operator.

This data is encrypted by vCloud Connector so, you can rest assured that your data will not be tampered with. The operator then imports your data into vCloud Air, and provides the same configurations and settings as per the on-premise datacenters.

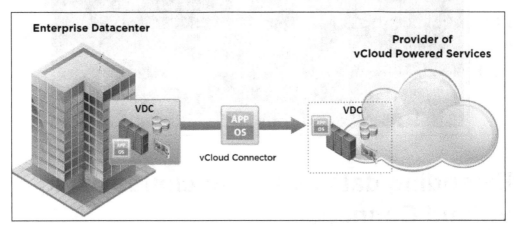

Image reference: http://www.vmware.com/files/pdf/vmware-vcloud-connector-technical-brief.pdf

vCloud Connector features

Let's have a quick look at some of the features of vCloud Connector:

- **Multi-cloud connections**: vCloud Connector enables you to connect your vSphere environments with your on-premise VMware vCloud Director, as well as with VMware-backed public clouds, such as vCloud Air, Bluelock, and StratoGen. It allows for seamless migration of virtual machines, vApps, and templates to and from various environments.

- **Unified management view**: Managing different VMware environments that are spread across private and public clouds can be a daunting task, especially when each provides a UI of their own. Using vCloud Connector, IT administrators can manage, deploy, and perform power operations on their diverse infrastructure all from a single pan of view. The management activities can be performed via a plugin for the vSphere Client interface as well as through a web-based UI.

- **Data center extension using Stretch Deploy**: Perhaps, one of the most important features of vCloud Connector—Stretch Deploy—allows the IT administrators to extend their on-premise datacenters into public clouds without the need to reconfigure the network settings of your virtual machines at the destination point.

While moving a workload, vCloud Connector stretches its private network boundary to the public cloud, so that it continues to get all its networking properties from the private network. In a way, your virtual machines thus retain their IP addresses, MAC addresses, NAT rules, and firewall definitions as they were provided on the private network.

- **Content Sync**: vCloud Connector Content Sync enables the IT administrators to synchronize and manage their entire content catalogs across various vSphere and vCloud environments. It basically allows you to have a master catalog called a Content Library which allows you to keep your templates all synced up across various environments.

  Using Content Sync, you can easily distribute your virtual machines, vApps, and templates across your organization while ensuring that the content remains the same across the environments.

Deploying vCloud Connector in your environment

Now that we understand the concepts and features of the vCloud Connector, let's see how to deploy it in your on-premise vSphere environment and later, look at how to connect our vCloud Air environment to it.

Here's a look at our demo environment. We have a small vSphere lab setup on a 198.19.99.0/24 subnet. The main purpose of this exercise is to demonstrate the ease by which you can connect and migrate a template from an on-premise vSphere setup to a vCloud Air organization using the vCloud Connector.

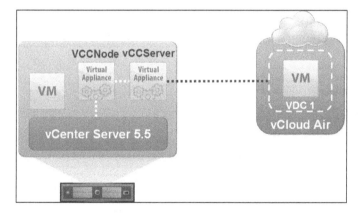

To start off, first download the vCloud Connector appliances from VMware. vCloud Connector consists of two components: a **vCloud Connector Server (vCCServer)**, and a **vCloud Connector Node (vCCNode)**. Download both the zip files to your local desktop, and unzip them to separate directories once the download completes.

 Note that you can install a vCloud Connector server in a vSphere environment or in a vCloud Director cloud. Download vCloud Connector vCCServer and vCloud Connector vCCNode from `http://www.vmware.com/products/vcloud-connector`.

Deploying vCloud Connector Server

Next, import the VCCServer vApp into your vSphere using the vSphere Client. Click on **File | Deploy OVF Template** to get started. This will bring up a wizard that will guide you through the deployment process.

Click on **Browse** and select the `VCCServer.ovf` file. Click on **Next** to continue with the deployment. There will be a set of screens that will ask you to accept the license agreement. Select the host on which you wish to deploy the OVF, as well as provide the necessary networking details for your vCCServer VM.

Provide a static **Network 1 IPaddress**, **Network 1 Netmask**, and **Default Gateway** in the **Networking Properties** window as shown, as per your vSphere environment's network settings. Make sure that this network is reachable on the Internet as well before you proceed with the next steps.

Networking Properties

Default Gateway
The default gateway address for this VM. Leave blank if DHCP is desired.

198.19.99.1

DNS
The domain name servers for this VM (comma separated). Leave blank if DHCP is desired.

8.8.8.8

Network 1 IP Address
The IP address for this interface. Leave blank if DHCP is desired.

198.19.99.245

Network 1 Netmask
The netmask or prefix for this interface. Leave blank if DHCP is desired.

255.255.255.0

Once done, you are now ready to deploy your vCCServer. Power On the VM from the vSphere client, and give the VM a couple of minutes to initialize. Once the VM is auto-configured, make a note of the URL that will be used to configure the vCCServer. The administrator web console will have a URL similar to this: `https://<vCCServer_IP_ADDRESS>:5480`.

Log in to the server Admin Web console with the username as `admin`. The default password is `vmware`. You can change this later on from the console itself.

Once logged in, you will be presented with a host of tabs on the main dashboard. Here's a quick round up of what each tab does:

- **System**: This tab provides general information about your vCloud Connector server. You can also configure your Connector's time zone, and also perform power operations for the VM.

- **Network**: This tab views network related information about the appliance. You can configure the vCloud Connector Server's IP address scheme proxy information here.

- **Update**: The **Update** tab allows you to check the update status of your virtual machine, and helps set your update policy.

- **Server**: The Server tab contains two sub-tabs: the **General** and **SSL** tabs. The General tab will provide you options to update the appliance's administrator password, adjust logging, and more. The **SSL** tab provides you with an option to upload and use your own SSL certificates for vCloud Connector. You can choose to ignore this tab for the time being; however, SSL certificates must be employed in vCloud Connector if you are using it on a live production environment.

- **Nodes**: The **Nodes** tab in the server **Admin Web** console lets you register vCloud Connector nodes with your vCloud Connector server. You can additionally download node log files, and register Stretch Deploy settings using this settings page. During the initial installation process, you can use this tab after you install the nodes.

Select the **Nodes** tab to view a list of currently added nodes for your vCloud Connector. By default, there will be only one entry here for the **Local Content Library** as shown in the following screenshot:

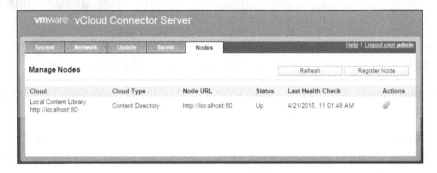

Deploying the vCloud Connector node

Next up, deploy the vCCNode OVF in a similar fashion as we performed for the vCloud Connector Server. Import the OVF into the vSphere Client, accept the license agreements, select the default ESXi host that will be used to deploy the OVF and finally, provide the network settings as required. Power on the VM after it is deployed, and give it a few minutes to initialize.

Once completed, you will be presented with the following screen. Make a note of the vCloud Connector Node's Web Console URL. The URL will be in `https://<vCCNode_IP-ADDRESS>:5480` form. Use the default username and password as provided during the vCCServer login.

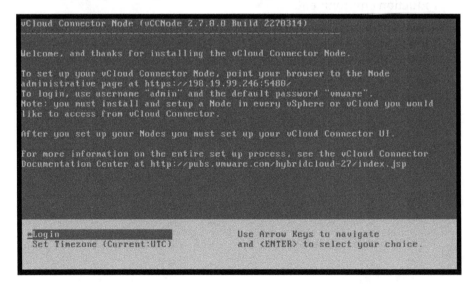

Once you are logged in to the vCCNode appliance, select the **Node** tab. The first task that we need to perform here is the registration of the vCenter Server/ vCloud Director with the vCloud Connector node.

To do so, select the Cloud tab and fill out the required fields as follows:

- **Cloud Type**: Here, you can select either the **vSphere** or **vCloud** option, according to your environment. In this case, we are connecting to our vSphere environment.

- **Cloud URL**: You can either provide your vCenter Server's IP address/ fully qualified domain name, or the vCloud Director URL as per your requirement.

- **Ignore SSL Cert**: This is an optional field; you can choose to enable this feature if you want to ignore the SSL certificates. SSL in enabled on nodes by default.

- **Use Proxy**: This is an optional field as well. You can select this option if your vCenter/vCloud Director is behind a proxy server.

Once all the necessary fields are populated with the correct values, click on the **Update Configuration** button. You will see the **Cloud Registration** updated info as shown here:

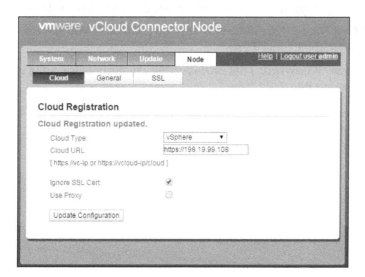

With our vCloud Connector Node setup for the vCenter Server, we now need to add this node to the vCCServer appliance. Log in to the vCCServer appliance and select the **Nodes** tab. Select the **Register Nodes** option to add our vCCNode Appliance.

This will bring up the **Register Node** with Server configuration utility as shown. Fill in the details as required and once done, click on the **Register** button to register the vCloud Connector Node with the Server. The following are the items under **Cloud Registration**:

- **Display name**: This provides a suitable name to identify your node; here, we have supplied the name Local vSphere.

- **Node URL**: This provides the URL of your vCCNode appliance.

- **Public**: Select this option in case the cloud that you are connecting to is a public cloud.

- **Use proxy**: This is an optional field. Use it in case there is a proxy server between the vCCServer and vCCNode.

- **Ignore SSL Certificate**: This is an optional field. Select this if you have not installed valid SSL certificates on your nodes.

Next, provide your vCenter/vCloud Director credentials as required:

- **Cloud Type**: You can either choose between **vSphere** or **vCloud Director** depending on your environment. In our case, we have selected vSphere.

- **VCD Org Name**: This field will only be enabled if you have selected **vCloud Director** in the **Cloud Type**.

- **Username/Password**: This provides the credentials for your vSphere environment here.

After the registration process completes, you will see the vCloud Connector Node listed under the Managed Nodes list. To edit the node's settings, click on the adjacent gear icon to edit the configurations as required.

Registering vCloud Connector in vSphere Client

As we discussed earlier, vCloud Connector provides two user interfaces: a plugin for the vSphere Client, and a web based admin console. In this section, we are going to see a few simple steps in which you can register vCloud Connector with a vSphere Client.

To begin with, log in to the vCloud Connector Server and select the **Server** tab as shown. Select the **vSphere Client** sub tab.

> Note that you can register the vCloud Connector user interface with only one vSphere Client at a time. To register with another vSphere Client, unregister, and then register with the new vSphere Client.

Furnish the necessary details as requested:

- **vCloud Connector Server URL**: In some cases, this field will be automatically populated; if not, then provide the vCloud Connector Server URL as appropriate
- **vCenter Server IP/FQDN**: This provides the vCenter Server IP address here
- **vCenter username**: This makes sure that the username you provide is a part of the administrator account, or at least has extension privileges for the vCenter Server
- **vCenter password**: This provides your vCenter user's password
- **Overwrite existing registration**: Select this option in case the vCenter Server has a vCloud Connector Server already registered that you want to replace
- **Use Proxy**: This is an optional field and is only required if the vCloud Connector Server has to pass through a Proxy to connect to the vCenter Server

Once completed, click on the **Register** button to register the vCloud Connector with vSphere Client.

When the registration is completed, a confirmation message will appear at the top of the page. To verify the registration, log in to the vSphere Client and select the **Solutions and Applications** tab from the **Home** page. You will see the vCloud Connector icon listed there.

Adding clouds to vCloud Connector

Now that we have our vCloud Connector server and Node setup, let's go ahead and add a few clouds to it. First, let's add the vCenter Server environment that we have prepped for vCloud Connector so far.

From the vSphere Client, select the **Solutions and Applications** tab from the **Home** page. Select the vCloud Connector icon listed there. You will see the **vCloud Connector dashboard** as shown next. You can browse through the various clouds that you add from the **Browser** tab on the left of the dashboard. To begin with, select the **Clouds** tab and click on the Add (**+**) button to add our vCenter Server.

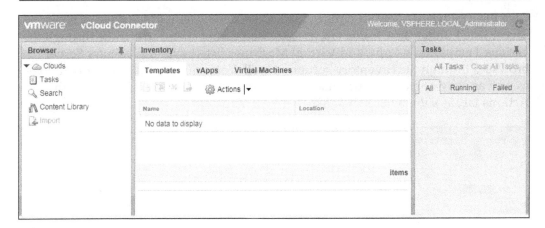

This will bring up the following dialog box. From the **Name** drop-down, select the name that you see there. This will be the display name that you provided during the registration of your vCloud Connector Node. The rest of the details should auto-populate as well, including the vCenter Server's URL. Simply, provide vCenter Server's user credentials and click on **Add** once done.

 For access to complete functionality, always use an administrator account or an equivalent role to add vSphere instances.

Give the dashboard a few seconds to load. Once done, you will see your vCenter Server listed under the **Clouds** tab, as discussed earlier. You can browse through the various **Templates**, **vApps**, and **Virtual Machines** listed with the vCenter Server by browsing through the **Inventory** section as well. You can perform power operations as well as copy or move virtual machines to other clouds by simply selecting the **Actions** tab, as shown here:

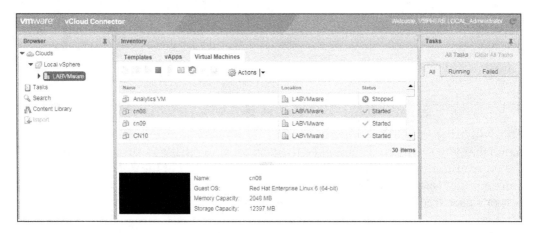

To register a vCloud Air organization with vCloud Connector, we'll follow the same steps as before, but with just one exception—there is no need for you to install a vCCNode appliance on your vCloud Air environment, as the vCloud Air vCCNode is already installed by VMware. You simply have to register the node with your on-premise vCloud Connector Server using your vCloud Air cloud credentials, and the VCCNode URL sent to you by VMware.

 At the time of writing this book, VMware did not send you the individual VCCNode URLs. You can use the following table as a reference for your respective VDC locations:

Location	URL	IP Address
Slough (UK)	`https://p6v43-vccmt.vchs.vmware.com:8443`	80.169.90.93
Virginia (USA)	`https://p4v54-vccmt.vchs.vmware.com:8443`	205.218.49.123
Santa Clara (California, USA)	`https://p3v29-vccmt.vchs.vmware.com:8443`	216.136.198.80

To register the vCloud Air VCCNode, log in to the vCloud Connector Server UI using the default credentials, select the **Nodes** tab, and then select the **Register Node** option. This will bring up the following dialog that will help you add your vCloud Air vCCNode. Provide a suitable Display name followed by vCloud Air vCCNode URL. Since this is a public cloud URL, we have selected the Public checkbox as well.

In the Cloud Credentials section, select vCloud Director from the drop-down, as shown next. Then, provide your VCD Org Name that you wish to connect to. This is the organization's name in the underlying vCloud air instance. Provide your user credentials, preferably the vCloud Air Account Administrator credentials. Once done, click on **Register** to complete the registration process.

Now that the registration process is completed, we can simply add our vCloud Air Organization to vCloud Connector using the vCloud Connector dashboard. Click on the Add (**+**) button, which will bring up the **Add Cloud** dialog, as shown next. From the **Name** drop-down list, select the **Display** name that you set for the vCloud Air organization. The **URL** field should auto-populate, as shown next. Provide your vCloud Air Account administrator credentials and click on **Add** once done.

Copying content between clouds using vCloud Connector

The IT administrators can easily copy virtual machines, templates, as well as vApps between the vSphere and vCloud environments that have been added to the vCloud Connector. vCloud Connector uses a streaming copy mechanism to export data from the source end to the destination. This streaming allows the data to be copied at a relatively high speed, as the data is made to flow parallel and in small chunk sizes rather than a single large, bulky file.

vCloud Connector also makes use of a staging area in the vCCNode appliance during the copy process, in case the import part of the copy process is slower than the export part. Hence, it is always a good practice to have sufficient space allocated to your vCCNode appliance, in case you are migrating large files.

 You can run a maximum of five concurrent copy tasks for on-premise nodes. There are no restrictions to the number of copy tasks that can be performed to public nodes (nodes in the public clouds).

In this scenario, we will copy a template (TINYLINUX) present on our local vSphere infrastructure over to the vCloud Air organization (VDC1). To begin with, log in to the **vCloud Connector** dashboard from the vSphere Client. Select the local vSphere environment, and select the **Templates** tab under the **Inventory** section as shown.

Before you begin with the actual copy process, make sure that these few prerequisites are met (structure it with relevant titles in bold):

- Ensure that the /VM/vApp template that you are copying over does not have any ISOs attached to it.

- Make sure that your /VM/vApp template has the latest set of VMware Tools installed and configured on it. In case you are copying over a Windows-based virtual machine, make sure it has the latest **sysprep** tools installed too.

- Make sure the destination catalog has write permissions.

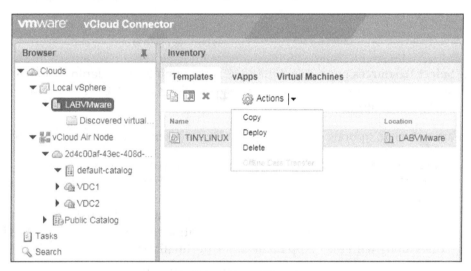

VCloud Connector ISO Inventory

To begin with the copy process, select any template that you wish to copy (in this case, we have selected the TINYLINUX template), and select the **Copy** option from the **Actions** drop-down menu.

This will bring up **Copy Wizard** that will walk you through the copy procedure. Provide a suitable **Name** and **Description** for your template. This will be the name by which the template will be created at the destination cloud.

Next, select the destination cloud to which you wish to copy this template. In this case, we are going to select the **vCloud Air Node** entry that we have registered earlier to our vCCServer appliance. Select the desired **catalog** that you wish the template to be copied to and once done, click on **Next** to continue.

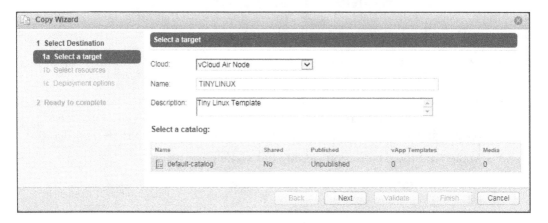

In the **Select Resources** page, select the VDC where you wish to deploy the new template. In our scenario, we are going to use the VDC1 (PRODUCTION VDC). Click on **Next** to continue.

There are two main options provided on the **Deployment options** page as shown:

- **Lossless copy**: This option is only valid when you are copying a vApp template from one vCloud Director to another. Since, in our case, our source is a vSphere and not a vCloud Director, we will not be using this option for now. An important thing to remember here though is that using this feature, you can preserve all the network configurations and the firewall and NAT rules along with the vApp name at the destination vCloud Director end.

  There are two downsides to this though: the first being that both the source and destination vCloud Directors must have identical vORGs (organizations), VDCs, and networks to work. The second issue being that you cannot use the **Deploy** option. You will have to deploy the vApp manually from the destination vCloud Director.

- **Deploy vApp after copy**: Selecting this option will provide you with some additional sub categories as described below:

  - **Network connection mode**: You can either choose **Direct** or **Fenced** depending on your requirements.

  - **Select network configuration**: Select a network for your vApp from the destination vCloud. In this case, we will be using **default-routed-network** (192.168.109.0/24).

° **Guest customization**: You can optionally choose to **Enable guest customization** for your vApp. Selecting this option will ensure that the vApp name and the network settings are configured for this template when it is powered ON at the vCloud Air VDC.

° **Change SID**: This is only applicable for Windows-based templates.

° **Allow local administrator password**: You can optionally provide and set a **Local administrator** password as well for your vApp. In our case, we have specified a password and also ensured that the administrator changes the password on the first login attempt.

° **Power on vApp after deployment**: This powers on the vApp, as suggested, after it has been deployed.

° **Remove temporary vApp template in destination vCloud catalog**: This removes the vApp template from the catalog in the destination cloud after the vApp has been successfully deployed.

Click on Next to continue.

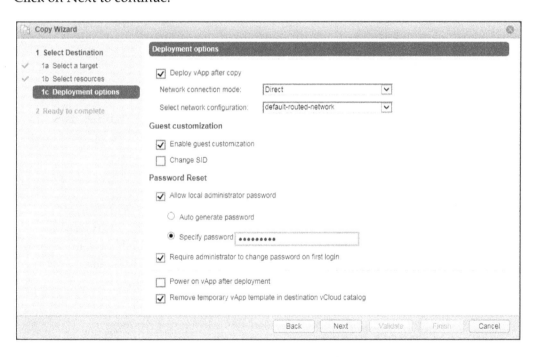

In the next page, review the configurations and select the **Validate** option to validate the settings. You may need to rectify or change certain parameters, in case you receive errors from the validation process. You can proceed with the copy operation only if the warnings are displayed. Click on **Finish** to start the copy process. You can view the status of the copy operation from the **Tasks** panel, to the right of the **vCloud Connector** dashboard.

Once completed, verify whether the template was successfully copied over to the destination, by logging on the vCloud Air dashboard and locating the vApp as shown here:

In similar ways, you can choose to copy over vApps and virtual machines as well. Just make sure that the objects have the latest VMware tools installed in them before proceeding.

Best practices and tips

- Make sure to set and open only the required firewall rules when working with VPNs. Follow this guide to setup a IPSEC VPN tunnel between vCloud Air and an on-premise environment securely—VMware KB article: 2051370.

- The vShield Edge Gateway must be configured to deny any unauthorized traffic to ensure that the remote site is fully secure.

- Make sure the vCloud Connector user has sufficient privileges to perform additional operations for the clouds. Ideally, use an organization administrator or a system administrator role for these activities.

- Ensure that the SSL certificates are present and valid before you copy/migrate any workload to and from the vCloud Connector in the production use.

- Monitor migration tasks at all times. Task information is available in the user interface for a period of 48 hours.

- Make sure that the vCCNode has adequate storage provided to it (by default it's 40 GB). You can resize the disk using the steps mentioned in this guide that is available at `http://pubs.vmware.com/hybridcloud-27/index.jsp`.

Summary

Let's have a quick recap of the things that we have covered in this chapter so far. We started off by revisiting the VPN services, and saw how easy and effortless it was to create secure VPN tunnels between two or more vCloud environments. Later on, we explored in depth the various features provided by vCloud Connector, and also saw how to deploy it on our on-premise infrastructure. We also learned how to extend the on-premise vSphere environment to vCloud Air using vCloud Connector and later, performed a simple copy operation to test its validity. In the next chapter, we are going to look at how we can monitor and manage our vCloud Air infrastructure using VMware vRealize Operations Suite of products.

5

Monitoring Workloads on vCloud Air

In the previous chapter, *Chapter 4, Extending vCloud Air*, we explored and learned various use cases for using a VPN tunnel to connect to a single or multiple vCloud sites. We also had an in-depth overview of VMware vCloud Connector, and saw how to connect and migrate workloads from an on-premise vSphere environment to vCloud Air.

In this chapter, we will be exploring a few advance topics that will show you how you can gain deep insights into your vCloud Air infrastructure and resources using a suite of products called as **vRealize Suite**.

The VMware vRealize Suite

The need to have a robust, all purpose, centralized management tool has become a true necessity now because more and more IT organizations are adopting the cloud. The current set of these tools either are too complex to setup and use, or simply operated in complete silos, thus not providing a clear picture about the growing operational or business requirements. IT companies are now looking for a single stack that can manage all aspects of an infrastructure environment; applications, physical hardware, virtualized platforms, and more, whether it may be and on premise or even hosted on a cloud.

With these issues in mind, VMware has developed a suite of products that come together to form the VMware vRealize Suite.

VMware vRealize Suite is a special management and automation solution built by VMware with the hybrid cloud specifically kept in mind. Although it is optimized for vSphere environments, the vRealize Suite can also be used to manage heterogeneous environments that may contain private clouds, such as OpenStack and public clouds, such as **Amazon Web Services (AWS)**; or simply have virtualized environments backed by **Microsoft hyper-V** and **RedHat KVM**.

Let's have a quick look at the services that vRealize Suite delivers:

- **Automated deployments**: vRealize Suite enables IT administrators to access their infrastructure using an easy-to-use, policy driven, self-service portal. It also provides the Administrators with the functionality to deploy infrastructure to any cloud environment using the concept of blueprints (master image). vRealize also helps to automate workload provisioning and deployment, as well as allocates the correct amount of resources to infrastructure based on the pre-deployed SLAs and business rules.

- **Intelligent operations**: vRealize Suite empowers the IT administrator to effectively and proactively manage overall infrastructure and application performance, monitor compliances and logs, as well as perform capacity planning and sizing operations as required. This enables the admins to drill down and perform root cause analysis on issues quickly, and perform the necessary remediation steps on time.

- **Business management**: In any business, it is essential that the IT administrator should be able to track and account for the workloads that are deployed either on the private or public cloud platforms. VMware vRealize Suite helps admins by providing interfaces using which they can charge the back departments, based on their resource consumptions. This enables business units to track the resource consumptions and avoid unnecessary costs and VM sprawls.

- **Unified management view**: vRealize Suite provides a unified view into the deployment and management of both: your on-premise infrastructure and a public cloud. IT administrators get a single pane of glass using which they are now able to track, provision, monitor, and manage lifecycles of virtual machines across the heterogeneous environments with ease.

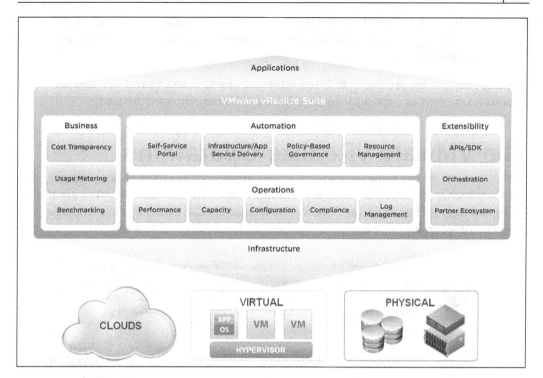

Image reference: `https://www.vmware.com/in/products/vrealize-suite/features.html`

VMware vRealize Suite comprises the following major components:

- **VMware vRealize Automation**: vRealize Automation provides a self-service portal, which IT admins can use to deliver applications and infrastructure resources in an on-demand basis. Using vRealize Automation, you can design, build, and configure standardized blueprints of your applications, and deploy them across hybrid clouds as and when required. vRealize Automation can also integrate and extend its functionalities with the existing configuration management tools, such as Puppet, Chef, and more.

- **VMware vRealize Operations**: vRealize Operations is primarily a health and performance monitoring solution that comprises of four VMware products, including the vRealize Operations Manager, vRealize Configuration Manager, **vRealize Hyperic**, and vCenter Infrastructure navigator. Using vRealize Operations, the IT admins can gain deep insights into their physical, virtual, and cloud-based infrastructure as well as applications. It can also be made to perform regulatory compliance management for PCI, SOX, HIPAA, and raise smart alerts in case the compliances are not met.

- **VMware vRealize Log Insight**: A part of the vRealize Operations suite, Log Insight provides real-time management of log data for all VMware environments.

For this chapter, we are going to learn more about vRealize Operations, and see how we can leverage it as a monitoring tool for our vCloud Air environment.

The VMware vRealize Operations

In this section, we are going to learn how to deploy vRealize Operations, in particular the vRealize Operations Manager, and configure it for high availability. We are then going to integrate the **vRealize Operations Manager**, also called **vROPs Manager**, with our on-premise vCenter Server and our vCloud Air environment.

 The VMware vRealize Operations Manager is shipped out as an OVA file, and can easily be downloaded from the VMware website for a 60 days trial period. You can download a copy from http://www.vmware.com/products/vrealize-operations/vrops-hol.

But before we go ahead and begin with the installation, let's take a quick look at some of the key components and features of vRealize Operations Manager.

The VMware vRealize Operations Manager can be installed in both of the following ways: as a standalone component as well as a scalable, clustered component. All the vRealize Operations Manager clusters contain one master node and can contain a few additional and optional data nodes. Let's look at the type of nodes provided by vRealize Operations Manager:

- **Master Node**: This is the first node that generally gets installed on the environment. It is primarily responsible for managing the cluster and all other nodes that will join to it later. In case you are planning for a standalone installation, then your Master Node will also act as the Data node, collecting various data metrics and perform analysis as well, single-handedly.

- **Data Node**: These are additional nodes that are deployed in large vSphere environments, and are responsible for data collection and analysis.

- **Replica Node**: This is used during the HA configurations; this node is a standard Data Node that replicates the Master Node.

- **Remote Collector Node**: This is an optional Node and is only responsible for gathering objects for the Operations Manager's inventory. These nodes do not store any particular data, or perform any analysis . They are generally used when the environment is dispersed and contains multiple deployments that can be separated by firewalls, and so on.

For our purpose, we will be deploying a fully functional cluster with Operations Manager HA enabled. In this scenario, we have a vSphere Lab that we will use to deploy the Operations Manager OVA file.

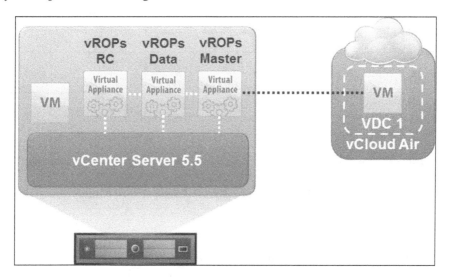

Once the OVA file is downloaded, import it into the vSphere environment using the vSphere Client. From the **File** menu, select **Deploy OVF Template**. Browse for **vRealize Operations Manager OVA** file and click on **Next** to continue.

Accept the license agreement and provide a suitable name in the **Name** field for this OVA deployment. In this case, it will be our Operations Manager Master Node.

Next up, from the **Deployment Configuration** page, select the type of deployment that you wish to have for your environment. Since this is a small environment with less than 2000 VMs, we have used the **Small** configuration. A complete list of the deployment configuration is shown here:

Deployment Configuration	CPU and RAM requirement	Number of VMs supported
Extra Small	2 vCPU	Only for the single-node, non-HA deployments
	8 GB vRAM	

Deployment Configuration	CPU and RAM requirement	Number of VMs supported
Small	4 vCPU	2000
	16 GB vRAM	
Medium	8 vCPU	2000-4000
	32 GB vRAM	
Large	16 vCPU	More than 4000
	48 GB vRAM	
Remote Collector (Standard)	2 vCPU	-
	4 GB vRAM	
Remote Collector (Large)	4 vCPU	-
	16 GB vRAM	

Select a suitable **Destination Storage** device for the deployment. In the **Disk Format** section, select the appropriate disk format as per your requirements.

 Snapshots can negatively affect the performance of a virtual machine, and typically result in a 25 - 30 percent degradation for the vRealize Operations Manager workload. Do not use snapshots.

In the **Properties** section, select your **Timezone** setting. By default, the time zone is set to UTC. You can use the UTC time zone in case the cluster nodes will be distributed across the different time zones.

Under **Networking Properties**, shown as follows, fill in the correct Default Gateway, DNS, Network IP Address, and **Network Netmask** as required. It's important to know that the master node and replica node require a static IP address. The data nodes or remote collector nodes may use DHCP or a static IP.

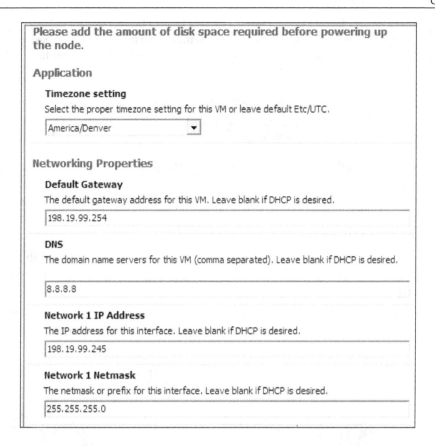

Once you have provided the necessary networking details, complete the OFA import process by selecting the **Finish** option. The OVA takes a couple of minutes to get copied over to the vCenter Server. Once done, simply **Power On** the virtual machine.

Select the **Console** tab and view the progress of the virtual machine as it powers up. Once the initialization is completed, you will see the vRealize Operations Manager Appliance welcome screen. Make a note of the Operations Manager Administration URL as shown here:

```
Welcome to the vRealize Operations Manager Appliance
To set up your environment, browse to one of the URLs provided below
and verify that the certificate's SHA1 thumbprint is:
CA:BC:80:09:2A:C7:02:A0:AF:1A:C7:81:5E:3E:B6:8B:11:F3:EE:AB

https://localhost.localdom/
https://198.19.99.245/
```

The appliance's hostname is defaulted to localhost. So as best practice, create a reference in your Active Directory prior to the vApp's deployment.

You will see the following screen. vRealize Operations Manager makes it really easy to install and configure multiple data nodes and extend the existing Operations Manager deployment, by using this wizard:

- **Express Installation**: As the name suggests, this is the fastest way to set configure the Operations Manager. The only configurable item during this phase of the configuration is the Operation Manager's administrative password. This installation will not help you setup HA or add any additional nodes to the existing Operations Manager.

- **New Installation**: This is the most frequently used option to install the Operations Manager. Using this option, you will be able to install and setup your Master Node.

- **Expand and Existing Installation**: This option is used to add additional Data Nodes or Remote Collectors to an already existing Operations Manager cluster.

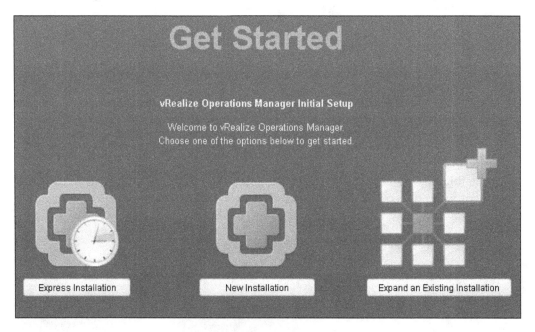

For the purposes of this exercise, select the **New Installation** option. This will bring up a wizard driven interface, as shown, using which, you will first setup your Master Node, follow the given steps:

1. Provide a suitable password for the Operations Manager administrator at the **Set the Administrator account password** screen. The user account name is admin by default, and cannot be changed. Click on **Next** to continue.

2. In the next section of the wizard, you can select whether to use the certificate included with vRealize Operations Manager or to install one of your own. To use your own certificate, click on **Browse**, locate the certificate file, and click on **Open** to load the file in the **Certificate** text box.

3. The file extension of the certificate file that you want to import does not matter. However, the certificate file must contain both: a valid private key and a valid certificate chain, and cannot be self-signed.

4. For this deployment, we have gone ahead and opted to use the default certificated, provided by the Operations Manager. Select **Next** to continue.

5. Next up, in the **Deployment Settings** page, provide a suitable name for **Cluster's Master Node**. In this case, we have provided the name as vROPs-Master.

6. Next, enter **NTP Server Address** based on your requirements. You can opt not to provide any NTP servers; in this case, the Data Nodes will sync to the Master Node virtual machine's local time. Click on **Next** to continue.

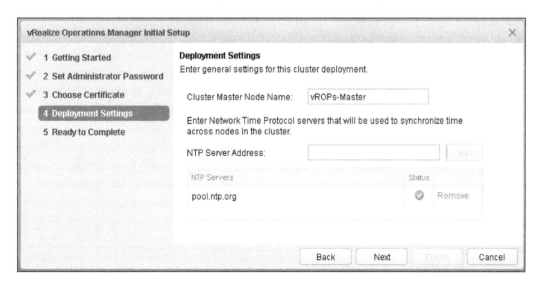

7. On the **Summary** page, verify your settings and click on **Finish** when done.

On completing the previous steps it will bring up the vRealize Operations Manager Administration dashboard as shown next. As you can see, the **status** of vRealize Operations Manager shows as **Not Started**. You can start up the service by selecting the **Start vRealize Operations Manager** option in case you are installing a standalone Ops Manager. For now, we will not enable this option.

You will also be able to view your Master Node under **Nodes**, in the vRealize Operations Manager Cluster. This is where all your Data Nodes, Replication Node, as well as Remote Collectors can be viewed enabled/disabled as well as deleted from the cluster.

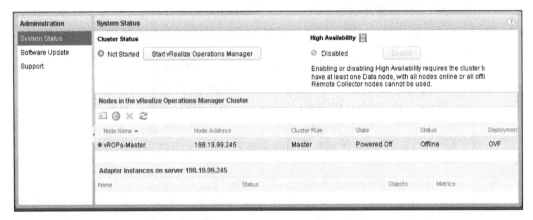

vRealize Operations Manager Administration dashboard

Adding the Data Nodes

Once the Master Node is all setup, we can now go ahead and add additional Data Nodes as required. The installation process is absolutely similar to the Master Node. Import the vRealize Operations Manager OVA into the vSphere environment and after the initial configurations, power on the appliance. Make a note of the Data Node URL that is shown in the **Console** tab as we did earlier.

Open a browser and add the Operations Manager Data Node URL in it. You will be shown with the same **Get Started** dashboard as we saw earlier during the Master Node configuration, follow the given steps:

1. Select **Expand an Existing Installation** to get started. This will bring up **Expand Existing Cluster** wizard. Click on **Next** to continue.

2. In the **Node Settings** and **Cluster information** page, provide a suitable name for your Node in the **Node** name field, as shown:

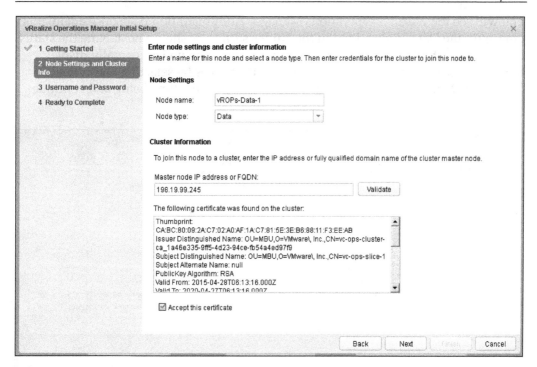

3. From the **Node type** drop-down menu, select **Data** as this will be our Data Node.

4. In the **Master node IP** address or **FQDN** field, type in the **IP address** of the Master Node. Click on **Validate** once done.

   This will bring up the Master Node's SSL certificate. Check the **Accept the certificate** and click on **Next** to proceed with the configuration.

5. In the **user name** and **password** page, you have two options to connect to the Master Node. You could either provide the cluster administrator's username and password, or choose to enter a passphrase that would have been provided to you by the Ops Manager administrator.

   In this case, we selected the option **use cluster administrator user name and password**. Click on **Next** once the credentials are filled in. Click on **Finish** to complete the Data Node addition.

You will see the vRealize Operations Manager Administration page once again; this time, with the Data Node added in the **Nodes** section as shown next. Note the status under the Cluster Role column. As you can see, both the nodes currently display their services as powered off. You can start the services by selecting Start vRealize Operations Manager, but we will leave this option for the time being and continue to add a Remote Collector to this cluster.

 You can add any additional Data Nodes as required using this same procedure.

Adding the Remote Collector Nodes

Remote Controller Nodes are actually optional and are not going to be required in your premise, unless you are running your vSphere environment in a dispersed fashion behind firewalls. Remote Controller Nodes neither store any data nor perform any analytics as their counterparts—the Data Nodes. These nodes are specifically designed to simply gather vSphere inventory objects for the Operations Manager's inventory.

Installing them is pretty much a similar process as compared to the Data Nodes. You start off by importing a vRealize Operations Manager OVA into your vSphere environment, provide a suitable name to it, configure its networking, and later deploy and power on the appliance. Follow these simple steps to get started:

1. Power on the vApp and select the **Console** tab to view its console. The vApp takes a couple of minutes to initialize. Once done, make a note of the vRealize Operations Manager Administration URL as done before.

2. From the **Get Started** dashboard, select the **Expand an Existing Installation** option. This will bring up the similar wizard that will guide you through the Remote Collector's configuration process.

3. In the node settings and cluster information page, provide a suitable **name** for the Remote Collector. In this case, we called it vROPs-Remote-1.

4. From the **Node** type drop-down menu, select the **Remote Collector** option.

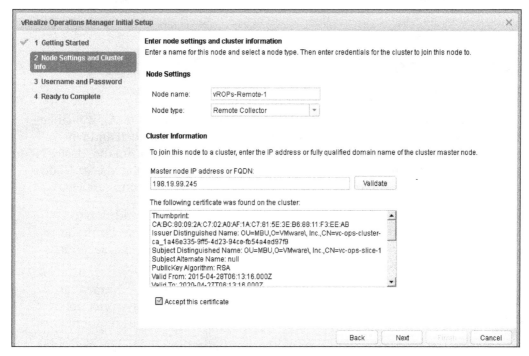

Setting up Remote Collector Node

5. In the **Master node IP address or FQDN** field, type in the **IP address** of the Master Node. Click on **Validate** once done.

   This will bring up the Master Node's SSL certificate. Accept the certificate and click on Next to proceed with the configuration.

6. In the **user name** and **password** page, provide the Operations Manager cluster administrator credentials. These are the same credentials that you have set during the Master Node's configuration phase. Complete the configuration by selecting the **Finish** option.

7. You will get redirected to the vRealize Operations Manager Administration dashboard as shown. You can view the recently added Remote Controller node under the **Nodes** section.

Nodes in the vRealize Operations Manager Cluster		
Node Name ▲	Node Address	Cluster Role
vROPs-Data-1	198.19.99.246	Data
vROPs-Master	198.19.99.245	Master
● vROPs-Remote-1	198.19.99.248	Remote Collector

Configuring HA for vRealize Operations Master Nodes

VMware vRealize Operations Manager supports high availability (HA) by enabling a Replica Node for the vRealize Operations Manager Master Node. If and when a problem should occur, the Replica Node kicks in and takes over from the Master Node with hardly a few minutes' worth of downtime, as the data from the Master Node is always replicated to the Replica Node. Follow the given steps to configure HA:

1. To enable HA, you must have a Data Node deployed in addition to the Master Node. Configuring HA is a very simple process. From the **vRealize Operations Manager Administration** dashboard, select the **Enable HA** option.

2. In the **HA Configuration** dialog box, select the Data **Node Name** that you added previously. Remember that in our case, we have only one Data Node; but you can have multiple, depending on your requirements.

3. The Data Nodes are listed in the **HA Configuration** dialog box. Select the Data Node that is most appropriate to your choice, as shown:

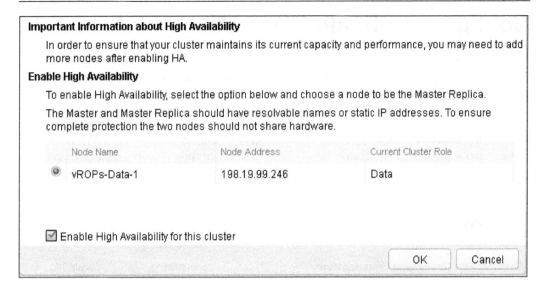

Important Information about High Availability

In order to ensure that your cluster maintains its current capacity and performance, you may need to add more nodes after enabling HA.

Enable High Availability

To enable High Availability, select the option below and choose a node to be the Master Replica.

The Master and Master Replica should have resolvable names or static IP addresses. To ensure complete protection the two nodes should not share hardware.

Node Name	Node Address	Current Cluster Role
vROPs-Data-1	198.19.99.246	Data

☑ Enable High Availability for this cluster

OK   Cancel

4. Remember to check the **Enable High Availability for this cluster** checkbox before proceeding. Click on **OK** to complete the configuration.

The HA configuration takes a couple of minutes to initialize the Replica Node. Once done, you will see the change in Cluster Role for your Data Node to Master Replica as shown:

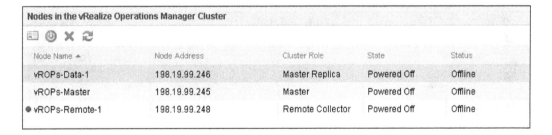

Nodes in the vRealize Operations Manager Cluster

Node Name ▲	Node Address	Cluster Role	State	Status
vROPs-Data-1	198.19.99.246	Master Replica	Powered Off	Offline
vROPs-Master	198.19.99.245	Master	Powered Off	Offline
● vROPs-Remote-1	198.19.99.248	Remote Collector	Powered Off	Offline

 Enabling HA when your cluster is active restarts the entire cluster.

Configuring vRealize Operations for the first use

Now that we have setup the HA and configured our Nodes, we are now ready to start the vRealize Operations Manager Service. Follow the given steps:

1. From the **vRealize Operations Manager Administration** dashboard, select the **Start vRealize Operations Manager** option, as shown. This will pop up a confirmation dialog box. The confirmation box ensures that you have adequate resources and Nodes present for your cluster before you enable it. Select **Yes** to start the application.

2. The application initialization takes a good few minutes to complete. You will see the status of your cluster change from **Initializing** to **Completed**. Once completed, you will be automatically re-directed to the **vRealize Operations Manager** login page as shown here:

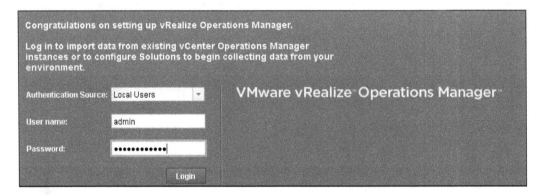

3. Log in to the vRealize Operations Manager using the same administrative credentials that were created and used during the Master Node's configuration. You will be prompted to accept and provide a few necessary details, such as **Acceptance of EULA**, entering a valid product license key if any, and more. Once done, your vRealize Operations Manager will be ready for use.

The vRealize Operations Manager is shipped as three different license models, each with their own sets of solutions acceptances:

- **Standard License**: This only allows for vCenter monitoring and management
- **Advanced License**: This allows for vCenter, and other infrastructure monitoring and management
- **Enterprise License**: This allows for all and any supported solutions, management/extension packs

The vRealize Operations Manager Solutions

Solutions provide views, alerting capabilities, reports, and a lot more features of a particular environment or application to the vRealize Operations Manager. Solutions can be delivered by vRealize operations Manager itself, or extended with the help of management packs. Management packs generally contain the same features as that of the solutions with an additional difference that they can contain adapters as well. Adapters can integrate vRealize Operations Manager with other third-party products and applications, such as an on-premise Infrastructure management tool like **IBM Tivoli**.

Configuring the vSphere Solutions pack

The most common solution pack that is shipped out with vRealize Operations Manager is the **vSphere Solutions** pack. This pack integrates vRealize Operations Manager with one or more vCenter Servers. Once connected, you can then monitor that particular vCenter Server's instances and perform operations on them.

The vSphere Solutions pack contains two adapters as explained here:

- **vCenter Adapter**: This adapter is used to connect and integrate the vRealize Operations Manager with a vCenter Server. You can have multiple vCenter Servers connected to a single Operations Manager. Each vCenter Server connection will require one vCenter Adapter instance to be configured for it.
- **vCenter Python Actions Adapter**: This adapter allows you to perform actions on the vCenter inventory objects.

Both of these adapters need to be configured in order for the vCenter Server to integrate with the vRealize Operations manager. To get started, log in to the vRealize Operations Manager UI, and select the **Solutions** tab as shown. You will see the vSphere Solutions Pack along with the two adapters as shown here:

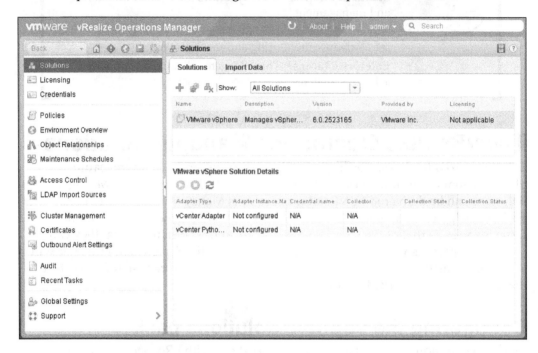

To connect a vCenter Server to the vCenter Adapter, follow the following steps:

1. Select **vCenter Adapter** in the **Adapter Type** list. Provide a suitable name in the **Name** field and optional description in the **Description** field for the adapter's configuration.

2. Next, in the **vCenter Server** text box, provide either the FQDN of your vCenter Server or its IP address.

3. Add the vCenter Server's administrative credentials by selecting the **+** sign next to the vCenter Server textbox. In the **Manage Credentials** dialog box as shown, provide a suitable name to identify the vCenter credentials. Enter the administrative **username** and **password** as applicable. Click on **OK** when done.

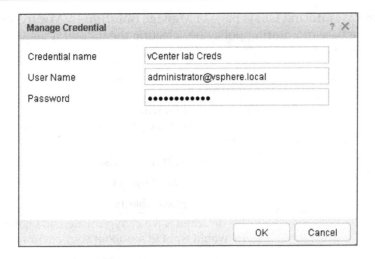

4. You can opt to test the connectivity as well by selecting the **Test Connection** option. You will get a vCenter Server certificate presented. Click on OK in the **Review and Accept the Certificate** dialog box as shown, to complete the connection.

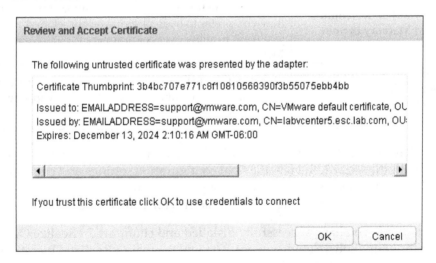

5. Click on **Save Settings** to save the vCenter Server credentials and configuration. With this, your vCenter Adapter will be ready to go!

Follow the same process to configure the **vCenter Python Actions adapter**. Once configured, you will be prompted to set the monitoring goals for your vSphere Solutions pack. This is a one-time activity and will not be available when you configure additional solutions.

On the **Define Monitoring Goals** page of **Manage Solution - VMware vSphere** wizard, create a base monitoring policy by selecting the following required options for your environment:

Option	Description
Which objects to you want to be alerted on in your environment?	This determines which objects you want to manage with the vRealize Operations Manager. There are three choices: • Infrastructure objects except virtual machines • Virtual Machines only • All vSphere objects
Which type of alerts do you want to enable?	This determines which type of alert and notifications you would want to see about your environment. You can choose either all or some of these options: • Health alerts • Risk alerts • Efficiency alerts
Do you want to overcommit CPU and Memory in your environment?	This determines how objects are monitored based on how you prefer to oversubscribe resources, and whether you want to allow over commitment for CPU and Memory.
Do you want to include Network & Storage I/O when analyzing capacity and workload?	This decides whether you want network and storage input, and output values included in your capacity calculations.

Once you have defined and created your basic monitoring goals, select **Next** to continue with the wizard. Review the final configuration settings and click on **Finish** to complete the vSphere Solutions Pack configurations. Both the adapters will now be ready, and will start collecting data and metrics for your vSphere environment.

Congratulations! You have successfully installed and configured vRealize Operations Manager for your vSphere environment. To view the main **vRealize Operations Manager dashboard**, select the home icon from. You will see the main dashboard as shown here:

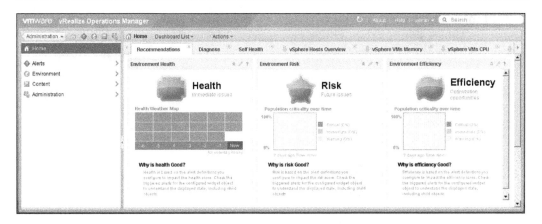

Configuring the vCloud Air Management Pack

As we have seen earlier, vRealize Operations Manager comes equipped with a wide variety of solutions and management packs to extend its monitoring and management to heterogeneous environments, including vCloud Air.

The vCloud Air Management Pack allows vRealize Operations Manager to collects metrics, change events, and resource topology information from your vCloud Air subscription. It displays this information on preconfigured widgets, such as vCloud Air top 25 VM performance graphs, heat maps, and more.

To get started, download the vCloud Air Management Pack from the VMware Solutions Exchange site. The download will be a compressed **TAR** file or a **PAK** file that needs to be imported into vRealize Operations Manager.

 You can download the latest copy of the vCloud Air Management Pack for free from https://solutionexchange.vmware.com/store/products/management-pack-for-vcloud-air-vch.

Once downloaded, log in to the vRealize Operations Manager using the administrative credentials and select the **Administrations** Tab | **Solutions** option to bring up the **Solutions** tab as shown. You can already see a VMware vSphere Solutions pack in use here.

To add the vCloud Air Management Pack, click on the + (Add) icon under the Solutions Tab as shown. This will bring up the Add Solution wizard. Using this wizard, we simply upload our new management pack and configure it for use.

Follow the given steps to add the vCloud Air Management Pack:

1. In **Add Solutions** wizard, select the **Browse** option. Browse for the downloaded tar of PAK file and click on **OK** to add it.

2. You can optionally choose to force the PAK file installation by selecting **Install the PAK file even if it is already installed** option. This will overwrite the settings and configurations of the PAK file in case they were previously installed.

3. Click on **Upload** to begin the upload process. This takes a couple of minutes to complete. You can view the upload process and verify whether it was successful or not as well. Once the PAK file is uploaded, it is now ready to be installed. Click on **Next** to continue.

4. Accept the license agreement and click on **Next** to continue. This will start up the installation process of the new management pack. Once the installation completes, click on **Finish** to close the **Add Solutions** wizard.

Your vCloud Air Management Pack is now ready to be configured.

Configuring the vCloud Air Management Pack is a very easy process. From the vRealize Operations Manager dashboard, select the Administrations tab. This will bring up the Admin dashboard for the Operations Manager. Select the Solutions tab to view the newly installed vCloud Air Management Pack as shown, and follow the given steps

1. Select **vCloud Air Adapter**. This will pop up the **Manage Solutions** wizard. You use this wizard to configure the adapters associated with solutions and management packs. Each adapter will have its own sets of requirements, which need to be configured using the **Manage Solutions** wizard. Once configured, the adapter will be able to communicate with the target system; in this case, the vCloud Air subscription.

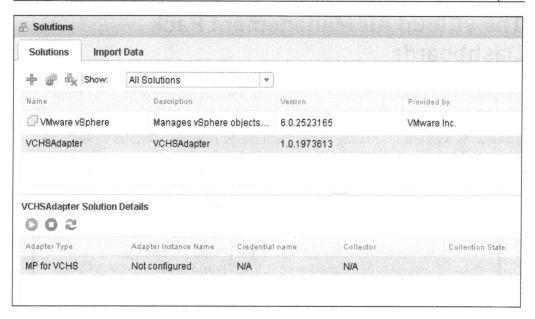

2. The first thing you need to configure is the **Display name** and the optional **Description** tab.

3. Next, in the **Credential** field, select the **+** (Add) sign to add your vCloud Air administrator credentials. Provide a suitable name for this set of credentials under the **Credential name** field. Next, provide a **user name** and **password** of your vCloud Air subscription. Click on **OK** to save the credentials.

4. Test the connection using the **Test Connection** option. Make sure the adapter can connect to your vCloud Air account before proceeding with the next steps.

5. Click on **Save Settings** to complete the adapter's configuration. The adapter will show **Collecting** as shown, under the **Collection State** column. This means that the adapter is successfully configured, and is able to collect data from your vCloud Air subscription.

The vCloud Air Management Pack Dashboards

Now that you have successfully configured the management pack, you can view the comprehensive dashboards to drill down into various aspects of your workloads on vCloud Air.

To view the vCloud Air Management dashboards, from the vRealize Operations Manager home page, select the **Dashboard List** drop-down menu as shown. You will see an entry called **VCHS** listed there. Under VCHS are the lists of sub-menus, each providing a unique insight into the overall performance of your vCloud Air subscription.

 At the time of writing this book, the vCloud Air Management Pack was yet to be renamed from **vCloud Hybrid Cloud Service (VCHS)**.

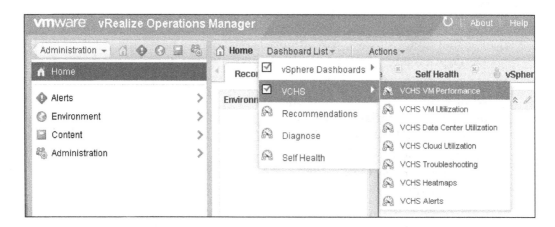

Here is a quick overview of each of the dashboards and the metrics that they support:

Dashboard Name	Description	Monitoring Metrics supported
VCHS VM Performance	This dashboard provides a list of the top 25 virtual machines that are network performance intensive	• SWAP in rate • SWAP out rate • Packets received per second • Packets transmitted per second

Dashboard Name	Description	Monitoring Metrics supported
VCHS VM Utilization	This dashboard displays the top 25 virtual machines based on different utilization parameters	• CPU usage • Memory usage • Disk usage
VCHS Data Center Utilization	This dashboard lists the top 25 data centers (VDCs) based on different utilization parameters	• CPU usage • Memory usage • Storage usage
VCHS Cloud Utilization	This displays the top 25 clouds based on different utilization metrics	• CPU usage • Memory usage • Storage usage
VCHS Heatmaps	This displays heatmaps of individual virtual machines present in each VDC	• CPU usage • Memory usage • Disk usage
VCHS Troubleshooting	This displays information regarding each object/ resource in vCloud Air in a hierarchical relationship	-
VCHS Alerts	This displays alerts regarding each object/ resource in vCloud Air in a hierarchical relationship	-

You can additionally install and configure vRealize Hyperic as well. Hyperic is an agent-based application and a performance monitoring tool that can be extended to vRealize Operations Manager using a Management Pack. Once installed and configured with vRealize Operations Manager, Hyperic provides a deep insight into the performance and overall utilization of a virtual machine's operating system, middleware, application, and more.

 You can find more information and use cases for vRealize Hyperic at
http://www.vmware.com/in/products/vrealize-hyperic/.

Best practices and tips

Following are the best practices:

- Create and use a custom user for the installation and configuration of vRealize Operations manager. Make sure that this user has sufficient administrative rights on the vCenter Server as well.

- Use SSL certificates wherever applicable, and set the time zone of each of the vRealize Operations Manager nodes correctly. The Nodes will not communicate with each other if they are out of sync with the time.

- Monitor resources and utilizations of VDCs as well as virtual machines. Ensure that you set correct threshold values and alert notifications for the same.

- Create custom thresholds based on your applications' needs. Leverage vRealize Hyperic to monitor your applications, such as SQL Databases, MS Exchange, Oracle, and so on.

Summary

Let's look at a quick summary of the things that we have covered so far. First off, we had a look at the vRealize Suite of products, and learned how we can leverage it to automate and monitor complex and heterogeneous environments. Next, we dived into vRealize Operations Manager, and set up a fully clustered, high enabled deployment containing a Master, a Replica and a Remote Collector Node. We then learned how to integrate different environments, such as VMware vSphere and vCloud Air with vRealize Operations Manager to leverage and create various dashboards, views, and alerts.

In the next and final chapter, we will be looking at disaster recovery—its uses, best practices, and how you can leverage VMware vCloud Air Disaster Recovery as a Service (DRaaS) offering in your own environment.

6
Business Continuity and Disaster Recovery using vCloud Air

In the previous chapter, *Chapter 6, Monitoring Workloads on vCloud Air*, we learned about the features and benefits of the VMware vRealize suite of products, especially the vRealize Operations Manager. We saw how to deploy a fully clustered and highly available Operations Manager, and later learned how to integrate it with both vSphere and vCloud Air environments using ready-to-use Solutions and Management packs.

In this final chapter, we will be exploring one of the most important functionalities and requirements of most of the enterprises today: business continuity and disaster recovery. We will learn the features and functionalities provided by VMware vCloud Air's Disaster Recovery service offering, and later see how to set up and test the same.

The importance of business continuity and disaster recovery

Unforeseen events such as natural disasters and calamities can bring the entire operations of an organization to a complete standstill. It is at this time that the Organization has to recover its day-to-day operations as quickly as possible and continue to provide services to their clients. Having a well-formed and tested business continuity and disaster recovery plan is an integral part of any organization's risk assessment and management.

 53 percent of the organizations can tolerate less than an hour of downtime before they experience a significant revenue loss or other adverse business impact, according to the ESG Research Review Data Protection Survey from the Enterprise Strategy Group.

Let's first try and understand the difference between disaster recovery and business continuity. Although both the terms are used quite often and interchangeably, they both are quite different from one another and their uses can vary from organization to organization.

Disaster recovery refers to the steps that are required to be carried out by an organization in case of a natural disaster or some form of emergency. These steps can include restoration of applications and servers from pre-taken backups, establishing network connectivity using redundancy, and so on. Business continuity describes a set of procedures that the organization has to keep in place to safeguard against a disaster. These steps ensure that all the critical applications and servers continue to perform and function even during a disaster. A good business continuity plan ensures that even during a catastrophic event, the organization can continue running its applications with minimal downtime, remain compliant, and protect their data at all times.

Let's have a quick look at some of the benefits that an organization can obtain by having a good business continuity and disaster recovery (BCP-DR) plan present:

- **Fast recovery**: A tested BCP-DR can help restore your applications and systems in a matter of minutes, ensuring the least amount of downtime of your day-to-day operations.

- **Reduce loss of service and revenue**: Certain businesses rely heavily on the uptime and availability of their applications, such as stock markets, manufacturing industries, and so on. An hour of downtime due to an emergency can cost potentially millions, and organizations risk losing their clients in the process as well.

- **Provide compliance benefits**: Certain compliances such as ISO, PCI, SOX, and HITECH mandate that an organization should have adequate strategies and services in place for protection against potential disasters.

The need for cloud-based disaster recovery

Traditional disaster recovery solutions generally involved replicating data and applications from an on-premise datacenter to an off-site remote location. Maintaining such facilities requires a lot of IT personnel and resources to undertake regular backups, maintain server hardware and storage devices, and more. Moreover, traditional disaster recovery is not a completely automated process, thus involving a lot of human intervention from time to time. This increases the overall time taken to restore data and applications, and can cost potentially millions to organizations.

As an alternative, many organizations are now turning towards cloud-based disaster recovery. Unlike its predecessor, cloud-based disaster recovery solutions do not need high initial investments in datacenters nor a suite of highly qualified personnel to operate and manage it. Using cloud-based disaster recovery options, the clients only have to pay for the storage and services that they consume. The clients also do not have to worry about overheads such as datacenter space, servers' uptime, connectivity issues, power supply, cooling, and more. These services are all abstracted and managed by the cloud provider itself.

Additionally, a cloud-based disaster recovery is also a highly automated and orchestrated process, which can be initiated within a matter of seconds as compared to the traditional DR. Automation also ensures that additional resources can be brought on, in case a disaster is detected and scaled down once the failback occurs.

Now that we understand the importance of a cloud-based disaster recovery solution, let's have a look at how you can leverage DR using your vCloud Air subscription.

VMware vCloud Air – Disaster Recovery

VMware vCloud Air - Disaster Recovery is a **Recovery as a Service (RaaS)** offering, provided by VMware to protect your on-premise workloads that can either be running on a vSphere or a vCloud Director-based platform.

Besides a vCloud Air - Disaster Recovery subscription, you will also require the following set of software for your disaster recovery to work:

- **VMware vSphere Replication**: VMware vSphere Replication is disaster recovery and protection software that can be integrated with an existing vCenter Server and vSphere Web Client to perform asynchronous replication of virtual machines. It can be integrated with different storage types, such as vSAN (Virtual SAN), traditional SAN, NAS, as well as direct attached storage (DAS). Once deployed, vSphere Replication can be used to copy your workloads to and from your on-premise vSphere infrastructure to a vCloud Air environment. You can optionally even configure additional parameters, such as network isolation and compression that can help data replicate faster and reduce the overall network bandwidth as well.

- **VMware vCloud Connector**: As discussed in the previous chapters, VMware vCloud Connector is a utility designed for easy migration of workloads to and from the different VMware environments. In this case, vCloud Connector is used primarily as an initial data seeding mechanism for offline data transfers.

In this chapter, we are only going to look at how to leverage **vSphere Replication** for disaster recovery with vCloud Air.

Key features and the benefits of VMware vCloud Air – Disaster Recovery

Let's have a quick look at some of the key features and benefits offered by VMware vCloud Air - Disaster Recovery:

- **Ease of getting started**: With vCloud - Disaster Recovery service, you do not need to bother about investing heavily in infrastructure or paying any upfront costs. You simply have to sign up for the disaster recovery service just as you would for the vCloud Air Dedicated Cloud or Virtual Private Cloud service, and start consuming your DR immediately.

- **Low costs and flexible**: Unlike traditional disaster recovery solutions, Cloud-based DR can scale according to the demands of your DR use case's varying requirements. These flexible options enable you to have adequate protection for your workloads as and when you require them. Also, you only pay for the services that you use. This significantly reduces both capital expenditure and operating expenditure costs, and enables organizations to provide better DR services.

- **Self-service based**: The entire DR process from start to end is under your control and can be managed using a single self-service based interface. You can either use the vCloud Air - Disaster Recovery web interface, or the on-premise vSphere Replication UI to start a replication process. Both the tools integrate seamlessly to allow for quick migrations.

- **Custom Recovery Point Objectives**: vCloud Air - Disaster Recovery allows users to provide their own **Recovery Point Objective** or **RPO** values per virtual machine. The RPOs can vary for a period of 15 minutes to 24 hours. Setting a unique RPO value per virtual machine allows for fine-grained control over replication frequency, based on business application priority.

- **Failover and failback through automation**: Unlike traditional DR solutions that require a lot of manual interventions, vCloud Air - Disaster Recovery provides automation and orchestration abilities with which you can trigger migration, failover, and failback of your virtual machines at any time you want. This is made possible using a tool called **vRealize Orchestrator**. You can integrate vCloud Air - Disaster Recovery with vRealize Orchestrator using a plugin and failover virtual machines in groups in specific order, thus giving you a lot of flexibility in your DR solution.

- **Multiple point-in-time recovery**: This is a new feature that is recently added to vCloud Air - Disaster Recovery. This feature allows you to failover your virtual machines to any of the 24 previous replication points in time. With multiple point-in-time recovery, you can select a specific point that you want to recover your data from, allowing you to successfully recover in the event of data corruption.

Setting up a disaster recovery service

VMware vCloud Air - Disaster Recovery is a core service similar to VMware vCloud Air Dedicated Cloud and Virtual Private Cloud services. You can start by signing up for the service using the VMware vCloud Air signup portal.

As a part of the enrolment process, VMware will set up a separate VDC, enabled for disaster recovery in vCloud Air. This VDC will serve as the replication target and recovery site. Once set up, VMware will then email your login credentials for the disaster recovery service.

> You can sign up for vCloud Air - Disaster Recovery service by simply filling out a form and submitting it to VMware at `http://vcloud.vmware.com/service-offering/special-offer`.

Here's a quick look at what vCloud Air - Disaster Recovery subscription has to offer:

Service component	Capacity
Computer	20 GB vRAM, 10 GHz vCPU
Storage	1 TB persistent storage
Bandwidth	10 Mbps
Public IP addresses	2 included + optional
Production support	24 x 7 x 365
Subscription terms	• 1 month • 3 months • 12 months • 24 months • 36 months

Once you have signed up, you can then use vCloud Air – Disaster Recovery to manage and monitor the replication process for your virtual machines. You can also perform various recovery tests and create placeholders for your virtual machines in vCloud Air in the event of a disruption at the source site.

VMware vCloud Air - Disaster Recovery also provides you with the added ability to customize and modify your VM's networking parameters as well. This ensures that your virtual machine has the same network configuration as it did on the source site. Once the VM is recovered to the cloud, you will be able to access it just as you would if the VM was on-site.

> You can access and operate your virtual machines recovered to VMware vCloud Air for the following periods of time:
>
> - 7 days to access and operate virtual machines when performing tests
> - 30 days to access and operate virtual machines when performing recovery

After the signup process is completed, log in to your VMware vCloud Air account using your credentials. On the main dashboard, you will see the **Disaster Recovery to the Cloud** option as shown here:

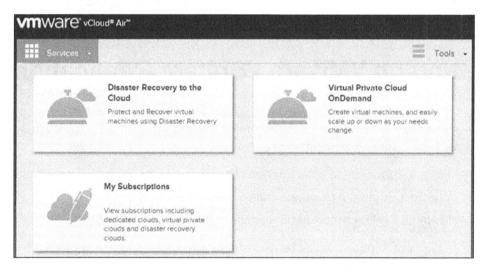

Just as with the Virtual Private Cloud service, vCloud Air - Disaster Recovery comes with two default networks: an external routed network that connects to the Internet, and an isolated network that is only accessible from within your vCloud Air - Disaster Recovery environment. You can use the isolated network during the testing of your virtual machine recovery from on-premise to vCloud Air as a test network, and use the external routed network during actual virtual machine recoveries.

You can create additional networks in your vCloud Air as well to support the test and actual recovery operations. But remember to create and update the target networks as well on the on-premise (source) site.

Besides the networks, you will also require the latest versions of VMware vSphere Replication and vCenter Server in order to configure them with vCloud Air - Disaster Recovery. A recommended product version table is shown here:

VMware product	Supported version
vSphere Replication appliance	6.0
vCenter Server	5.5.x and above
ESXi host	5.0, 5.1.x, 5.5.x, and 6.0
vSphere Web Client	6.0

Once your vCloud Air - Disaster Recovery account is all set up, we can proceed with the installation and configuration of the VMware vSphere Replication at an on-premise VMware vSphere environment.

Setting up VMware vSphere Replication

VMware vSphere Replication is an extension of VMware vCenter Server that is a quick and easy hypervisor-based virtual machine replication and recovery. It is designed to protect virtual machines from failures by replicating the virtual machines between the following sites:

- From a source site to a destination site
- Within a single site from one cluster to another
- From multiple source sites to a shared remote destination site

VMware vSphere Replication can be downloaded as a ready-to-use appliance from the MyVMware portal. Each appliance contains three important components: a vSphere Replication Manager server, an embedded database, and a plugin for the vSphere Web Client.

 You can download an evaluation copy of vSphere Replication at https://my.vmware.com/web/vmware/evalcenter?p=vsphere6.

Once downloaded, import the appliance into your vCenter Server using the following steps:

1. Log in to the vSphere Web Client and select **vCenter | Hosts and Clusters**.

2. Select an **ESXi** host that you wish to deploy the vSphere Replication appliance on. Right-click on the host and select the **Deploy OVF template** option.

3. Select the **Browse** option to browse for the vSphere Replication OVF file and click on **Next** when done.

4. The next few steps are pretty self-explanatory. Click and accept the **Accept the End User License Agreement (EULA)** and provide a suitable name in the **Name** field for your deployment.

5. Select **cluster, host** or **resource pool** for where you want to deploy the OVF template. Click on **Next** when done. Finally, provide a suitable static **IP address** and other network configurations for your deployment. You can alternatively choose to provide a DHCP-based IP address but ideally, you should provide a static IP. Next, provide a suitable password for the appliance's administrator account. Click on **Next** to continue.

6. Review the configurations and click on **Finish** to complete the import process. The OVF takes up to a minute or two to get imported into the vCenter Server. Once imported, go ahead and power on the appliance.

Once the appliance is powered on, it will automatically integrate itself with the vSphere Web Client. You will need to log out and log back into the vSphere Web Client, in order to view the vSphere Replication plugin on the dashboard as shown in the below image:

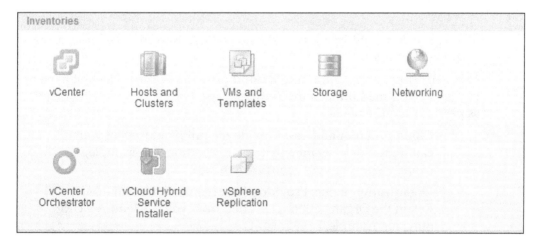

Configuring a vSphere Replication connection with vCloud Air

In this section, we are going to look at some simple steps by which you can add your vCloud Air - Disaster Recovery subscription to vSphere Replication.

From the vSphere Web Client, select the vSphere Replication icon to get started. On the **vSphere Replication** dashboard, you will see three tabs up front: **Monitor**, **Manage** and **Deploy**. Let's have a quick look at what each tab contains, and what it can be used for:

- **Monitor tab**: This tab displays the current set of ongoing replication tasks, issues, and logs. You can list the outgoing and incoming replication jobs and their status using this tab.

- **Manage tab**: As the name suggests, you can manage your target (destination) sites using this tab. You can additionally list the replication servers, and perform basic connectivity operations on them as well using this tab.

To start off, let's select the **Manage** tab and then select the **Target Sites** option. You will see two icons listed on the dashboard. The first icon will help you add a vCenter Server as a target site. This vCenter Server can either be the same vCenter Server to which the vSphere Replication is attached, or a completely different one. The second icon will help you add a cloud provider as a target site. We will use the **Add a Cloud provider** option to add our vCloud Air - Disaster Recovery subscription account.

Follow these steps to add your own vCloud Air - Disaster Recovery subscription to vSphere Replication:

1. Select the **Add Cloud Provider** icon to set up a new vCloud Air connection as discussed earlier.

2. This will bring up the **Connect to a cloud provider** wizard. The first page to be displayed is the **Connections Settings** page. Fill up the following details as per your requirements:
   - **Cloud provider address:** Provide the full IP address of your cloud provider. Retain only the URL portion, for example, `https://p2v12-vcd.vchs.vmware.com`.
   - **Organization name:** Provide your organization's name here. Retain the Organization ID portion from your vCloud Air URL only; for example, `88887650-123`.

- ○ **Credentials**: In the **Credentials** tab fill up your vCloud Air **Username** and **Password**. The connections will be validated once you click on the **Next** button to proceed. Make sure the validation shows successful before proceeding.

3. The next page will provide you a list of VDCs that you can select to connect your vSphere Replication with. In the **Virtual Datacenters** page, select the appropriate virtual datacenter as per your requirements. Click on **Next** to proceed.

   Once again, a validation will take place to verify the VDC's connection to vSphere Replication. Make sure the validation is a success before proceeding.

4. Verify the connections and cloud provider settings in the **Ready to complete** page. Once done, click on **Finish** to complete the cloud provider addition.

The cloud provider addition takes a couple of minutes to complete. Once done, you can verify the connectivity by selecting the **Manage** tab on your **vSphere Replication dashboard** as done earlier. You will now see your newly added cloud provider listed there.

Make sure the **Status** field shows connected. Mostly, this field will show a status as **Missing network settings**. This is because you first need to specify the networks that vSphere Replication should use to test and recover virtual machines from on-premise to the cloud.

We have already discussed how vCloud - Disaster Recovery creates a routed and isolated network during initialization. During a test recovery, vSphere Replication will use one of these test networks to replicate the virtual machine on. Ideally, it is good practice to have both, the test and actual recovery networks created separately.

To configure the networks, select the **Missing network settings** link on the vSphere Replication manager dashboard. This will pop up a **Configure Target Networks** wizard as shown here:

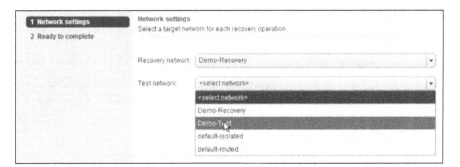

From the drop-down list, select the appropriate network you want to use as **Recovery network** and **Test network**. Note that these networks have been created and configured for vCloud Air—Disaster Recovery. Click on **Next** to proceed with the wizard. Review the settings on the **Ready to complete** page and click on **Finish** to complete the network configuration.

With this configuration done, you have now added your vCloud Air successfully with the on-premise vSphere Replication. Now if you perform either a test or an actual recovery operation with vSphere Replication, the recovered virtual machines on vCloud Air will automatically get attached on either the test or recovery network as per your requirement.

Configuring the virtual machine replication

Once your vSphere Replication is integrated with your vCloud Air - Disaster Recovery subscription, you can now go ahead and configure virtual machine replication from on-premise to the cloud. Follow these simple steps to get started:

1. Log in to your vCenter Server using vSphere Web Client and select the **Host and Clusters** tab to view your virtual machines.

2. Select a virtual machine that you wish to replicate over to the vCloud Air. Right-click on the virtual machine's name and select the **All vSphere Replications Actions** option. Select the **Configure Replication** option. This will bring up the **Configure Replication** wizard as shown:

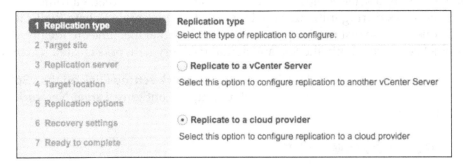

3. Select the **Replicate to a cloud provider** option and click on **Next** to continue.

4. In the **Target site** window, select the previously configured vCloud Air - Disaster Recovery site that we had configured. This will be the target site where the virtual machine replication will take place. Click on **Next** to proceed with the wizard.

5. Next up, in the **Target location** window, select the appropriate storage policy that you wish to configure for your virtual machine at the target (vCloud Air) site. There are two options provided here. You can either use the standard storage policy provided by VMware vCloud Air, which is either use SSD-Accelerated drives or standard drives; or you can choose to use replication seeds.

6. Replication seeding is a method used for transferring virtual machines from a source to a target site that are simply too big in size, or consume a lot of the network bandwidth. Seeding a virtual machine at the target site can be achieved by the following methods:

    ° Offline data transfer: Using VMware vCloud Connector's offline data transfer feature, you can export a virtual machine as a packaged OVF file, and then import it into vCloud Air as a virtual machine.

    ° Cloning the virtual machine: You can even create a virtual machine seed by cloning it inside a VDC.

    ° Copying over a network: Use some other method besides vSphere Replication to copy over a virtual machine from the source over to the target site.

   In this case, we have not opted for replication seeds. Select an appropriate storage policy as required for your virtual machine and click on **Next** to proceed.

7. The next window provides certain **Replication options** that you can configure, depending on your virtual machine. One of the options provided is **Guest OS quiescing**. This is an optional feature, and you can opt to ignore it for the time being. However, in case you are replicating a Windows OS based virtual machine, then you can select **MS Shadow Copy Service (VSS)** as the quiescing method as shown. Click on **Next** to continue.

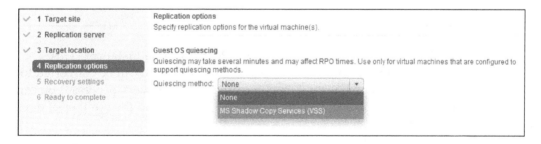

8. On the **Recovery settings** page, select the RPO metric that you want to specify for your virtual machine. The **Recovery Point Objective (RPO)** metric indicates how much data you are willing to lose in case of a disaster.

9. You can use the RPO slider or the time spinners as shown, to set the acceptable period for which the data can be lost in the case of a site failure. VMware vSphere Replication currently supports a RPO range from 15 minutes to a maximum of 24 hours. Since we are replicating a small Linux machine in our case, we have set the RPO to a modest 4 hours. The RPO value that you set can greatly depend on factors such as the size of your virtual machine, the available bandwidth between the source site, the target site (in this case, the target site is VMware vCloud Air), and more.

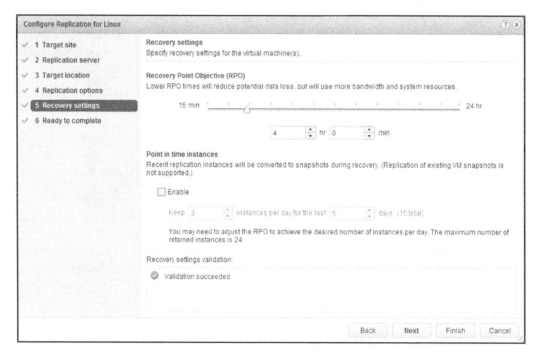

10. Another feature of vSphere Replication is **Point in Time instances**. This feature is used to save multiple replication instances that can be converted to snapshots of the source virtual machine during the recovery process. You can even select the number of instances you wish to keep and the number of days as well.

 You can keep up to 24 Point in Time instances of a single virtual machine.

11. Once your RPO value is set, click on **Next** to proceed with the replication wizard.

12. Review the replication settings for your virtual machine in the **Summary** page and click on **Finish** to complete the replication wizard process.

To verify the replication process status, select the **vSphere Replication** tab from the vSphere Web Client dashboard. Select the **Monitor** tab. On the **Monitor** Tab, go to **vSphere Replication** tab and view the status of the virtual machine in the **Outgoing replications** list.

Performing the virtual machine test recovery

Test recoveries can be performed in two ways. You can trigger a test recovery from either the vSphere Replication manager or from the vCloud Air - Disaster Recovery UI. Let's first have a look at how we can trigger a test recovery by using the vSphere Replication manager; follow the given steps:

 Before you progress with a test recovery, remember that you need to have at least one replication task configured, as we performed in the previous section of this chapter.

1. From **vSphere Web Client**, select the **vSphere Replication** icon. This will bring up the **vSphere Replication** dashboard. On the main page, select the **Monitor** tab.

2. Next, select the **vSphere Replication** tab to list the available virtual machines for the test recovery procedure. You will see a virtual machine listed here from our last activity.

3. Select a particular virtual machine that you want to test and then select the **Run Test Recovery** icon. The **Run Test Recovery** icon is a blue play button located in the tool bar, above the listed virtual machine.

4. This will pop up a **Test Recovery** wizard. Before proceeding with the test recovery, you will need to authenticate against the vCloud Air environment. In the **Connections settings** page, provide the **Username** and **Password** of your vCloud Air account. Note that the **Cloud provider address and the Organization name** field are already auto-populated.

5. Click on **Next** to proceed with the wizard.

6. In the **Test Recovery** options page, select the appropriate recovery option and click on **Next** to continue. By default, there are two options provided:

   ° **Synchronize recent changes**: You can use this option to synchronize the data of the source virtual machine before the test recovery is actually run.

   ° **Use latest available data**: This option is used when you do not want to synchronize the data. In this case, the latest available copy of the virtual machine instance will be used for the test recovery.

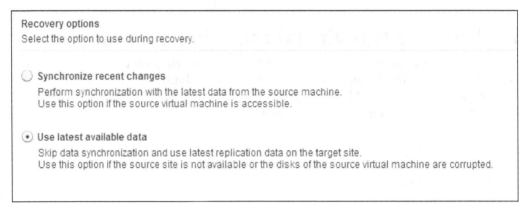

Test Recovery options page

7. Once done, click on **Next** to continue. In the **Ready to complete** page, review the changes and click on **Finish** to start the test recovery process.

You can view the status of the synchronization process in the **Monitor** tab of the vSphere Replication dashboard. The status will show a green tick indicating a successful synchronization. Next, log in to the vCloud Air account and select the **Disaster Recovery** tile to open up the disaster recovery dashboard. Here, you will see a **Virtual Machines** tab. Select the tab to view the test recovery virtual machine. By default, this virtual machine will be in a powered-off state. You can power it on by selecting the **Actions** tab, followed by the power on option as shown:

Once the test recovery is successfully conducted, it is also equally important to clean up the same. You can only run a test recovery or a planned migration activity for a replication after the results of the previous test recovery are all cleaned up.

To perform a test, perform the following steps:

1. First up, from the vCloud Air dashboard, power off your running test recovery virtual machine. You can do this by selecting the **Virtual Machine Details** tab; select the **Settings** tab, and then click **Power Off**.

2. Next, run the test cleanup operation from the **vSphere Replication** interface. Select the **Monitor** tab and click on the **vSphere Replication** option. Select the **failover virtual machine** and then click on the **Run Test Cleanup** icon.

3. In the **Test Cleanup** confirmation box, select **Yes** to clean up the test recovery results for the selected virtual machine from the target site.

4. With the cleanup now complete, you can navigate back to your vCloud Air - Disaster Recovery dashboard and verify the status of your virtual machine. It will have changed from **Test** state to **Placeholder**.

With this, you have successfully configured and run a test recovery, followed by a test cleanup as well.

VMware vCloud Air Data Protection

Besides the traditional vCloud Air - Disaster Recovery service, VMware also provides an optional business continuity solution using VMware vCloud Air Data Protection. In this section, we are going to have a brief look at what vCloud Air Data protection service is and how you can leverage it for your environment.

To begin with, vCloud Air Data Protection was formerly a vSphere product suite, designed for taking image level backups of virtual machines and virtual appliances. Today, the product does the same thing but more or less with the vCloud Air environment. It leverages EMC's Avamar product's technology to perform agent less virtual machine backups to disk.

Let's have a quick look at some of vCloud Air Data protection's features and benefits:

- **Self-service portal**: You can configure backups of all your virtual machines and vApps using a single self-service based portal. The Data Protection tool is installed and configured on an on-premise datacenter, but it can manage and schedule backups for virtual machines that reside on the vCloud Air platform as well.

- **Integration with EMC Data Domain Systems**: Since vCloud Air Data protection is based on proven EMC Avamar technology, it can easily be integrated and extended to work with other EMC-based software to increase the overall backup efficiency.

- **Application aware backups**: vCloud Air Data protection supports application aware backups for a host of business critical applications, such as Microsoft Exchange, Microsoft SQL Server, and Microsoft SharePoint. For example, in case a user's mailbox seems corrupted, you can use Data protection to restore that individual mailbox.

- **Changed Block Tracking (CBT) restore**: vCloud Air Data protection leverages either a full block restoration process or changed block restoration process, depending on the virtual machine's needs and requirements. Often, the best mechanism is selected to ensure optimum performance and efficiency.

You can purchase a subscription for the Data Protection service through the My VMware portal. Once your subscription is activated, you can begin consuming it using the vCloud Air dashboard. Here's a quick look at the subscription model for both: the vCloud Air Dedicated Cloud service as well as the Virtual Private Cloud Service:

Service Component	vCloud Air — Dedicated Cloud	vCloud Air - Virtual Private Cloud
Data protection capacity	1 TB persistent storage	1 TB persistent storage
Number of backup jobs	Unlimited	Unlimited
Number of restore jobs	Unlimited	Unlimited
Concurrent backup jobs	16	16
Concurrent restore jobs	16	16
Production support	24 x 7 x 365	24 x 7 x 365
Subscription terms	<ul><li>1 month</li><li>12 months</li><li>24 months</li><li>36 months</li></ul>	<ul><li>1 month</li><li>3 months</li><li>12 months</li><li>24 months</li><li>36 months</li></ul>

Once you have subscribed to vCloud Air Data Protection, you can start consuming its service in a similar way as the vCloud Air - Disaster Recovery service. You can additionally even set policies for data protection and ensure that your virtual machines meet the required protection needs.

Data protection provides two different ways in which you can apply policies:

- **To entire VDCs**: This is also called as the **Enabled Mode** in Data protection. Using this method you can ensure that all the virtual machines within the specified VDC are protected automatically. By default, the entire VDC backup occurs everyday between 6:00 and 10:00 UTC time. The backups are retained for a period of 30 days. These values can be customized from the **Data Protection** tab in your vCloud Air dashboard.

- **To vApps directly**: This method is also called as a **Self Service Mode**. Using this method, you will have to individually choose which virtual machine you would like to assign the particular policy to. This is a completely manual process as Data Protection will not back up all the virtual machines of your VDC automatically. Similar to the VDC backup, the individual vApps can be restored to any point for 30 days by default.

You can disable backups and restore jobs, set customized retention periods, and reset the data protection policies at any time. Remember, you will be required to have at least the virtual administrator privileges in vCloud Air to enable and configure Data Protection for your VDCs and vApps.

Best practices and tips

Here are a few simple best practices that you should keep in mind when designing or building disaster recovery services using vCloud Air:

- Assess your applications and plan for disaster recovery. Not all applications are alike and not all of them have a similar RPO as well. You can group applications that have some common traits then create disaster recovery plans and SLAs specifically for them.

- Be prepared for a disaster at all times. Run periodic disaster recovery tests from your on-premise to vCloud Air and vice versa. Remember to document the process as well.

- Make sure you have an adequate and dedicated bandwidth to perform a disaster recovery. A poor bandwidth connection to your vCloud Air can have a negative impact on the virtual machine's RPO and RTO.

- Keep a disaster recovery always simple if you want it to work out well. Designing and maintaining a simple, concise disaster recovery plan will increase your chances of a successful failover and recovery.

Summary

In this chapter, we learned about the importance of having a tested and implemented disaster recovery and business continuity plan. We also learned a bit about the traditional disaster recovery model and its drawbacks; we learned how the cloud has changed the entire DR paradigm by providing faster, cheaper, and more efficient DR services. Next, we explored VMware vCloud Air's Disaster Recovery service, its key features and benefits. We also saw how easy it was to set up virtual machine recovery and data replication to VMware vCloud Air using vSphere Replication and Data Protection. Last but not the least, we learned a few essential best practices that you should always keep in mind when designing and building your very own disaster recovery solution.

Index

A

Amazon Web Services (AWS) 122

B

best practices and tips, vCloud Air 85, 118
business continuity
significance 148
business continuity and disaster recovery
(BCP-DR) plan
benefits, to organization 148

C

catalogs 27
characteristics, cloud computing
cost effective 3
flexible services 3
multi-tenancy 2
resource pooling 2
robust and reliable 3
Cisco 88
cloud-based disaster recovery
need for 149
cloud computing
about 2
characteristics 2
cloud computing, uses
burst compute capacity 4
Dev and Test 4
disaster recovery 4
temporary sites 4
components, VMware vRealize Suite
VMware vRealize Automation 123
VMware vRealize Log Insight 124
VMware vRealize Operations 123

custom catalogs
creating 46-49

D

Data Nodes 130
disaster recovery
significance 148
disaster recovery service
about 7
best practices 165
setting up 152-154
vCloud Connector 8
vSphere Replication 8

E

Early Access Program (EAP) 8
Enabled Mode 165

F

features, vCloud Connector
Content Sync 103
data center extension, using
Stretch Deploy 103
multi-cloud connections 102
unified management view 102

G

gateways
about 57
networking services 71
golden image 27

H

HA
  configuring, for vRealize Operations
    Master Nodes 134, 135

I

IBM Tivoli 137
Infrastructure as a Service (IaaS) 3
interface, VMware vCloud Air
  gateways 15, 16
  gateways, properties 15
  navigating through 12
  networks 16, 17
  resource usage 13, 14
  virtual machines 14
Internet
  virtual machines, connecting to 64-71

J

Juniper 88

M

Microsoft hyper-V 122
multi-site VPN connectivity
  about 93-100
  Local Networks 98
  Peer Network 98

N

network
  about 58-61
  Default-Routed-Network 16
  Isolated Network 17
  virtual machines, connecting to 63
networking components, vCloud Air
  about 56
  VMware vShield Edge 56
  VXLAN 56
networking services, gateways
  about 71, 72
  DHCP 72, 74

  Firewall 76
  load balancing 79
  load balancing, scenarios 80-85
  NAT 74, 75
  static routing 77, 78
  virtual private networks 79
networking topologies, connecting
  enterprise site to vCloud environment 88
  multi-site vCloud environments 88
  single-site vCloud Environment 88
nodes, vRealize Operations Manager
  Data Node 124
  Master Node 124
  Remote Collector Node 125
  Replica Node 124

O

Offline Data Transfer (ODT)
  deploying 101
Open Virtualization Format (OVF) 27
Operations Manager OVA file
  deploying 125-127

P

PAK file 141
Platform as a Service (PaaS) 3
public IPs
  assigning 61, 62

R

Recovery-as-a-Service (RaaS) 7
Recovery Point Objective (RPO) 151
RedHat KVM 122
Remote Controller Nodes
  adding 132-134
roles, VMware vCloud Air
  account administrator 21
  network administrator 21
  read-only administrator 21
  subscription administrator 21
  virtual infrastructure administrator 21

Thank you for buying
Learning VMware vCloud Air

About Packt Publishing

Packt, pronounced 'packed', published its first book, *Mastering phpMyAdmin for Effective MySQL Management*, in April 2004, and subsequently continued to specialize in publishing highly focused books on specific technologies and solutions.

Our books and publications share the experiences of your fellow IT professionals in adapting and customizing today's systems, applications, and frameworks. Our solution-based books give you the knowledge and power to customize the software and technologies you're using to get the job done. Packt books are more specific and less general than the IT books you have seen in the past. Our unique business model allows us to bring you more focused information, giving you more of what you need to know, and less of what you don't.

Packt is a modern yet unique publishing company that focuses on producing quality, cutting-edge books for communities of developers, administrators, and newbies alike. For more information, please visit our website at www.packtpub.com.

About Packt Enterprise

In 2010, Packt launched two new brands, Packt Enterprise and Packt Open Source, in order to continue its focus on specialization. This book is part of the Packt Enterprise brand, home to books published on enterprise software – software created by major vendors, including (but not limited to) IBM, Microsoft, and Oracle, often for use in other corporations. Its titles will offer information relevant to a range of users of this software, including administrators, developers, architects, and end users.

Writing for Packt

We welcome all inquiries from people who are interested in authoring. Book proposals should be sent to author@packtpub.com. If your book idea is still at an early stage and you would like to discuss it first before writing a formal book proposal, then please contact us; one of our commissioning editors will get in touch with you.

We're not just looking for published authors; if you have strong technical skills but no writing experience, our experienced editors can help you develop a writing career, or simply get some additional reward for your expertise.

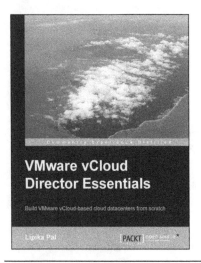

VMware vCloud Director Essentials

ISBN: 978-1-78398-652-1   Paperback: 198 pages

Build VMware vCloud-based cloud datacenters from scratch

1. Learn about DHCP, NAT, and VPN services to successfully implement a private cloud.

2. Configure different networks such as Direct connect, Routed, or Isolated.

3. Configure and manage vCloud Director's access control.

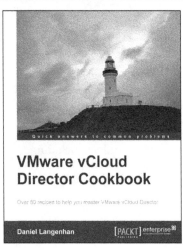

VMware vCloud Director Cookbook

ISBN: 978-1-78217-766-1   Paperback: 364 pages

Over 80 recipes to help you master VMware vCloud Director

1. Learn how to work with the vCloud API.

2. Covers the recently launched VMware vCloud Suite 5.5.

3. Step-by-step instructions to simplify infrastructure provisioning.

4. Real-life implementation of tested recipes, packed with illustrations and programming examples.

Please check **www.PacktPub.com** for information on our titles

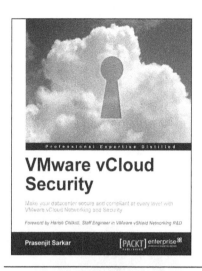

VMware vCloud Security

ISBN: 978-1-78217-096-9   Paperback: 106 pages

Make your datacenter secure and compliant at every level with VMware vCloud Networking and Security

1. Take away an in-depth knowledge of how to secure a private cloud running on vCloud Director.

2. Enable the reader with the knowledge, skills, and abilities to achieve competence at building and running a secured private cloud.

3. Focuses on giving you broader view of the security and compliance while still being manageable and flexible to scale.

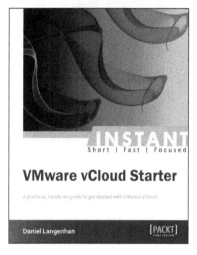

Instant VMware vCloud Starter

ISBN: 978-1-84968-996-0   Paperback: 76 pages

A practical, hands-on guide to get started with VMware vCloud

1. Learn something new in an Instant! A short, fast, focused guide delivering immediate results.

2. Deploy and operate a VMware vCloud in your own demo kit.

3. Understand the basics about the cloud in general and why there is such a hype.

4. Build and use templates to quickly deploy complete environments.

Please check **www.PacktPub.com** for information on our titles